I0418625

HENNY'S BOAT

The Maritime Rescue Operation that Saved Denmark's
Jews and Sparked a Nationwide Revolt Against the Nazis

Howard S. Veisz

This work is a new and expanded edition of the book, titled *Henny and Her Boat, Righteousness and Resistance in Nazi Occupied Denmark,* which was originally published by the author in 2017.

ISBN: 979-8-9857224-0-6 (Paperback Edition)
ISBN: 979-8-9857224-2-0 (Hardcover edition)
ISBN: 979-8-9857224-1-3 (eBook Edition)

Library of Congress Control Number: 2022905816

Copyright © 2022 Howard S. Veisz
All rights reserved

Without limiting the rights reserved above, no part of this publication may be reproduced, stored in or introduced into any retrieval system, or transmitted, in any form or by any means (electronic, mechanical, photocopying, recording, or otherwise), without the written permission of the author.

To contact the author, write to hennysboat@gmail.com.

Cover photograph by Joe Michael, Mystic Seaport Museum.

TABLE OF CONTENTS

PREFACE

In October 1943, after occupying Denmark for three and one-half years, the Nazis set a plan in motion to capture all of the country's Jews in a single night and send them on the path to annihilation. With seventy-two hours to go, a member of the Nazi occupation staff disclosed the plan to one of Denmark's political leaders. The disclosure triggered a nationwide rescue effort that was unique in occupied Europe. Within twenty-four hours, the Danish people mobilized to warn and hide their Jewish countrymen. When Gestapo agents fanned out on their overnight raids, they came up almost empty-handed. The chase, however, had just begun. The only possible destination that the Gestapo could not reach was unoccupied Sweden, and the only way to get there was by crossing the *Øresund*—the body of water that separates Denmark from Sweden—by boat. Almost overnight, groups sprang up along the Danish coast to organize escape routes on fishing boats and other craft. Hundreds of boats participated. Few if any made as many crossings and saved as many people as *Gerda III*, a forty-foot workboat owned by the Danish Lighthouse and Buoy Service.

Henny Sinding, the twenty-two-year-old daughter of the Service's commander, teamed up with the crew of *Gerda III*, and with members of a fledgling resistance group, to save at least three hundred Jews from the Nazis. Every day and night for a month,

Henny engaged in the dangerous business of meeting Jews at secret rendezvous points around Copenhagen and escorting them to a warehouse attic overlooking the boat. Carefully evading Nazi sentries who patrolled the docks, she then led the Jews, one by one, into *Gerda III*'s cargo hold. Each morning, *Gerda III*'s four-man crew completed the escape—travelling fourteen miles or more past German warships and mines to Swedish ports. From a dark recess inside the warehouse, Henny watched *Gerda III* head to sea before she left to get a few hours of sleep and prepare to gather more Jews who were waiting to be rescued.

During October 1943, *Gerda III* made daily covert crossings, and Henny made hundreds of clandestine trips through the darkened late-night streets of wartime Copenhagen, with Jews who were being hunted by the Gestapo.

Gerda III was part of a fleet, estimated to include up to three hundred Danish boats, that set out from more than forty ports, fishing villages, and seaside towns to rescue Denmark's Jewish population. Together, these vessels and their crews saved at least 7,742 Jews, nearly 95% of the Jews living within Denmark. The Jews who were rescued included many whose families had been part of Danish society for centuries, and others who had recently fled to Denmark from Germany and other countries where rising anti-Semitism made life unbearable.[1] Another 686 non-Jewish family members were transported with them.[2]

As the Jewish rescue operation wound down, the resistance group that Henny had become a part of remained united. Energized and emboldened by their success in the rescue, its members—consisting mainly of university students and a few navy cadets who joined their ranks—transformed the group into one of Denmark's most daring and effective sabotage rings. For more than three months, beginning on October 28, 1943, the group conducted sabotage missions throughout Denmark, blowing up factories and other facilities that aided the Nazi war machine. Month by month their targets grew larger, their operations more complex, and their risks greater—culminating in a raid that verged on the impossible.

Some members of the group were killed, some were captured, and others—including Henny—escaped to Sweden using escape routes similar to the ones they devised to save Jews a few months earlier.

The formation of the *Gerda III* rescue group and its transformation into a hard-hitting sabotage ring exemplifies—on an exceptional scale—the surge of resistance activities that swept Denmark in the autumn of 1943. Although a resistance movement was stirring in the months before the Nazis attempted to deport and exterminate Denmark's Jews, the rescue catapulted the resistance to a level far beyond what it had been and what it might otherwise have become. Resistance organizations took shape almost overnight. People who had remained on the sidelines stepped forward and proved themselves. Routes devised to rescue Jews became conduits for moving resistance fighters and weapons across the Øresund. By banding together to save their Jewish countrymen, Danes took a major step toward saving Denmark itself.

After Henny and other survivors of her group escaped to Sweden, *Gerda III* remained behind, its crew continuing the dangerous business of carrying Nazi targets to safety. Over the remaining fifteen months of war, *Gerda III*'s hidden passengers consisted mainly of Danish resistance fighters whose identities had been exposed, members of their families, and British and American airmen who were forced to land crippled warplanes or parachute from them onto Danish soil. Making clandestine crossings several times each week after the Jewish rescue operation was completed, *Gerda III* saved another six hundred to seven hundred people from the Nazis.

When the war ended, *Gerda III* remained in the Danish Lighthouse and Buoy Service for another forty-one years.[3] After it was replaced by a newer vessel named *Gerda IV*, and began to suffer the inevitable decline of a retired workboat, *Gerda III* itself was rescued. The Danish government donated *Gerda III* to the Museum of Jewish Heritage in New York, which brought it back to life with the help of supporters on both sides of the Atlantic. Today, *Gerda III* is based on Connecticut's Mystic River, where the wooden boat experts at the Mystic Seaport Museum care for and display the vessel on behalf of the Museum of Jewish Heritage.

The boat today is exactly as it was during its wartime missions.[4] In her hull and on her decks, the presence of both the rescued and the rescuers is palpable. The small cargo hold where Henny hid ten to fifteen Jews during each passage still carries their spirit—and hers. Across a bulkhead from the cargo hold where fleeing Jews, resistance fighters and Allied airmen huddled, the massive two-cylinder semi-diesel engine that propelled *Gerda III* and her human cargo during the war years is kept in running order and is started from time to time. The engine runs at a slow, steady pace, the firing of its cylinders sounding more like a rapid heartbeat than the drone of a modern diesel. In the windowless cargo hold, where each beat of the engine meant a little more progress toward Sweden and a little more confidence that life would go on, you can feel fear giving way to hope and then to joy.

Viewing *Gerda III* from its Seaport dock, you can imagine the boat tied to the berth that Henny arranged behind the warehouse where she gathered Jews in the attic. Step back a few meters, the length of the gap between *Gerda III* and the warehouse gate, and you can view *Gerda III* as those refugees first viewed her—at a time when the boat embodied their hopes of getting out alive.

Peering over *Gerda III*'s bow, you can begin to imagine what it was like for those waiting and watching on the other side of the Øresund for more refugees, possibly loved ones left behind, to reach Sweden. That scene was poignantly described in a Swedish newspaper account:

> We are standing on the beach, watching the dark waters…
> Will anybody cross tonight?
> Will they escape the hunt taking place on the other side? And suddenly you hear a throbbing from somewhere, the sound of a motor… The bow of a ship appears through the fog. People are crowding the deck…. Slowly the boat approaches, the pale faces of the passengers are all directed

toward the harbor...some petrified and some radiant with happiness. But on the faces of all of them you read fatigue, a bottomless feeling of fatigue and resignation. And suddenly the tension is relieved. Someone onboard starts singing [the Swedish national anthem]. And everybody joins.... They only remember a word here or there of the text, but nevertheless...they join in a mighty chorus.... Here they come, hunted from home and house, driven from their jobs and sometimes torn away from their relatives, and here they come singing as if they were approaching the gates of Paradise.... The boat draws alongside the quay. A Swedish officer calls out a hearty 'Welcome.' The refugees hurry on land with their small bundles. Many fight to keep back their tears.... One kneels and kisses the soil of Sweden.[5]

Of the hundreds of boats that took part in the rescue of the Danish Jews, *Gerda III* is believed to be one of only three that remain afloat.[6] A fourth rescue boat is on permanent display within the halls of the United States Holocaust Memorial Museum in Washington, D.C. No others are known to exist.

Gerda III is a powerful embodiment of the Danish rescue and a tangible link to the extraordinary people associated with it—Henny; Mix, a dashing naval cadet and resistance fighter who quickly became her soulmate; the *Gerda III* crew members who served the resistance in multiple ways; and other giants of the Danish resistance—who displayed unwavering heroism and humanity in the face of evil. Their story epitomizes the story of the Danish people. It is the story of a nation that rose from a humbling surrender to battle the Nazis and hand the Gestapo its most glaring defeat. And it is compelling proof of what good people can accomplish when they resolve to combat bigotry and oppression.

Chapter One

HENNY: COMING OF AGE
IN A TIME OF WAR

HENNY SINDING WAS EIGHTEEN in April 1940, the month the Nazis invaded her country. Seven months earlier, Nazi Germany's invasion of Poland triggered the start of World War II. But Denmark had remained neutral, and at peace, until now.

Henny went to bed on the night of April 8 in a free and independent Denmark and awoke the next morning to find that a predawn German invasion had not only taken place, but had already succeeded. It was all over in two hours.

Shortly after 4:00 a.m. on April 9, German tanks and other military vehicles rumbled across Denmark's southern border into the Jutland Peninsula, Denmark's largest land mass, and raced through the peninsula with little opposition. By 4:30 a.m., German troop ships landed invasion forces in Zealand, Denmark's largest island and the home of its capital, Copenhagen. Soon after the amphibious landings had begun, German paratroopers opened another invasion route by capturing the Storstrøm Bridge, at the southern tip of Zealand, in the world's first airborne assault. As soon as the bridge was secured, German troops raced across it toward Copenhagen. (Two hours later, paratroopers captured the Aalborg Airfield in the north of Jutland, providing German warplanes with a base for launching attacks on

1

Norway.) By 5:00 a.m., German forces had reached the gates of Copenhagen's Amalienborg Palace, where the king was meeting in emergency session with his foreign minister, military chief, and other members of the government. And at 6:00 a.m., amidst a gun battle between the invasion forces and the Royal Guards protecting the Palace, the king ordered his military to stand down. Guns fell silent at the Palace and throughout the rest of the country. Before most Danes started their workday, the framework of a permanent cease fire, and an open-ended occupation, had already been agreed upon.

Henny stepped out of her house that Tuesday morning onto streets and under a sky that were filled with the unmistakable signs of Nazi conquest. German troops patrolled the streets in force, and German bombers circled overhead. The nightmarish scene was compounded by propaganda leaflets—messages from Hitler addressed "to the Soldiers and the People of Denmark"—that carpeted the sidewalks. Another young Dane named Leo Goldberger, whose father was the cantor of Copenhagen's Great Synagogue at the time, recounted in later years how the green leaflets fell "like confetti" from German planes that "blackened the sky" as they "roared" overhead. Reaching out from a window of his family's apartment, not far from Henny's home, he caught a leaflet as it wafted by. In it he read that "strong German forces have since this morning taken possession of the most important military objectives in Denmark and Norway" and would be staying for the duration of the war in Europe. People throughout Copenhagen read the same message.[7]

Absurdly portraying the invasion as an act of friendship rather than war, the leaflets asserted that Nazi Germany had "decided to take over the protection" of Denmark, and that "from now on, the German Army and Fleet would ensure the security of [Denmark] against English aggression." The leaflets further asserted that agreements "currently being reached on these measures" between the German and Danish governments, would guarantee that the "freedom of the Danish people is respected and that the future independence of [Denmark] is fully secured."

Making an instant mockery of those assurances—and getting to the real point—the leaflets went on to state that "until these negotiations are concluded, it must be expected that the [Danish] Army and the Fleet…as well as the people…refrain from any passive or active resistance." Any attempts to resist, the leaflets warned, "would be useless and would be broken" by the overwhelming power of Nazi Germany's armed forces. The bottom line, as the Danish king and his government ministers had already concluded, was that armed resistance would be both futile and deadly for the Danish people.

Denmark's government had made its peace and accepted the presence of German troops on Danish soil. In the interest of preserving Danish lives, it asked its citizens to do the same.

As Leo Goldberger summed it up:

> We were urged [by the Germans] to go about our daily business as usual—as if nothing had happened. And indeed, after an emotional appeal on the radio by the prime minister and our beloved old king—Christian X— we did just that.[8]

For the next three years, Henny did as her government urged, notwithstanding her hatred of the Nazi invaders. She continued to lead her life, as did nearly all of her countrymen, much as it existed before the invasion. While war raged elsewhere in Europe, Henny's life continued to be shaped largely by her love of the Danish coast and her family's attachment to it. She was, in her words, "mad about everything that had to do with the sea."[9] She was born into it and was never far from it.

Henny, the second of three children of Chika and Paul Sinding, was born on August 8, 1921. She began life in a navy enclave within Copenhagen at a time when her father was a young naval officer. Officially called *Nyboder* (Danish for New Barracks), the row houses that comprise the enclave are more commonly and accurately known as the Yellow Houses. They were new in the seventeenth century when King Christian IV built them to house the sailors and junior officers of the expanding Royal Danish Navy. The newest buildings were added in the mid-eighteenth century and, outwardly, little has changed since then. Following long standing tradition, the picturesque row houses continue to be painted the same shade of yellow as the Royal Dockyard buildings across the harbor, and to be adorned with red tile roofs, red shutters, and green doors. Inside the homes, as Henny knew them, were spartan living quarters that reflected the buildings' age and military origin.

As her father's stature in the navy improved, so too did their accommodations. When she was five years old, Henny's family moved across the harbor to Christianshavn. There they lived in an attractive yellow house facing the tree-lined Christianshavn Canal, a picturesque side channel that parallels Copenhagen's long inner harbor. The walls of her home were decorated with seascapes that her father, a talented artist in his spare time, painted in his attic studio. Copenhagen remained just a short walk away, across a bridge that spans the inner harbor and the stone wharfs that line its shores.

A young Henny at the tiller.
(Photograph courtesy of the Sundø family.)

Henny, following in the footsteps of the father she adored, took to sailing as a young girl. As she grew older, the strait between Denmark and Sweden, known as the Øresund, became Henny's playground and her refuge. In her teenage years, she began to race sailboats at the Hellerup Sailing Club on the northern outskirts of Copenhagen, and she became good at it. In time she graduated from sailing dinghies to Dragon sloops, sleek thirty-foot vessels of Norwegian design that were raced in Olympic competition for more than two decades after the war. With a strong sense of adventure, and well-founded confidence in her abilities, rough weather rarely kept Henny from venturing out under sail. Far from being deterred by the challenge of guiding her boat safely through cresting seas and stiff winds, she thrived on it. At the tiller she was the very picture of focus and determination. Those traits, coupled with her knowledge of the Øresund, the streets of Copenhagen, and the Christianshavn waterfront, would serve her well in the coming struggle.

During the year of the invasion, Henny went to work for the Danish Lighthouse and Buoy Service, the navy unit that her father commanded. Each day, she reported to the Service's headquarters at the Royal Dockyards, the homeport of the Danish Navy since the seventeenth century. At her Dockyards office, Henny kept the Service's nautical charts current by marking shifts in buoy locations, entering the location of wrecks—the number of which rose steadily during the war, as floating mines took their toll on vessels motoring along the Danish coast—and recording other hazards to navigation.

The docks immediately outside her office were wartime berths for lightships that had been taken out of service after the German invasion, and for the lighthouse tender *Gerda III*—a workboat that went to sea every day in war and peace. Fourteen years earlier, in 1926, the Service built *Gerda III*, a forty-foot vessel made of oak and pine, to work the Øresund's often rough and sometimes icy waters. *Gerda III*'s four-man crew maintained buoys that guided ships through the Øresund. And it made daily trips, carrying supplies, mail, and lighthouse keepers between the Service's headquarters and the Drogden Lighthouse, an imposing structure that served then, as it does now, as a beacon and a traffic control center for vessels entering and leaving the Baltic. Since 1937, lighthouse keepers have stood watch from a vantage point one level beneath the light, monitoring ships transiting between the broad expanse of the Baltic and a narrow deep-water channel through the Øresund (the Drogden Channel), which leads to the North Sea and, beyond it, the Atlantic.

*Gerda III in July 1943, three months before the
start of the Jewish rescue operation.
(Photograph courtesy of the Dines Bogø Archive.)*

Although Henny was not a member of *Gerda III*'s crew, she worked with the crew members and spoke their language. As Henny and the crew became well acquainted with one another, a kinship formed between them. *Gerda III*'s crew became part of Henny's extended family, just as the Lighthouse and Buoy Service was very much the family business. Henny was there each morning when *Gerda III* headed out to sea, and she was there when it returned.

Beyond the confines of the Lighthouse and Buoy Service, the expansive Dockyards evoked Denmark's proud past as a Baltic Sea power, able to dominate its adjacent seas and project force to holdings across the Atlantic. But it also presented a searing portrait of the loss, by any conventional measure, of the power that Denmark once possessed.

For more than a century, Denmark's sway over the Baltic had been slipping away, sapped by the dissolution of a four-hundred-year union with Norway, and by territorial losses to Sweden and Germany.[10]Although the Dockyards continued to be ringed by Danish military vessels of various sizes and descriptions, Denmark's naval and land forces had been eclipsed by the rise of European superpowers—none more so than neighboring Germany—with far greater populations, land mass, and resources. Denmark's weakened position was sealed by a 1935 Anglo-German Naval Agreement that allowed Germany to expand its navy beyond the limits imposed upon it at the end of World War I—an agreement that Winston Churchill castigated in Britain's Parliament for giving Germany "absolute command of the Baltic." That reality was driven home during the invasion, when German warships disembarked invasion forces at multiple points along the Danish coast with impunity, and steamed into Copenhagen, while Denmark's naval guns remained silent. Germany's command of the seas around Denmark would have been evident to a bright young woman like Henny—a woman who divided her time between the Royal Dockyards and the family home of a Danish naval officer.

But, while Denmark's conventional power had slipped away, it cultivated strength of a different kind—an inner strength. Danes were steeped in the principle that their nation's enduring strength rested on twin pillars: robust democracy and the unbreakable commitment of its people to stand up for that democracy and for each other. It was a type of strength that might not enable Denmark to repel invaders at the border, but would enable Danes to outlast them and emerge with Denmark's fundamental values intact.

Those were pillars around which Denmark drew a line, refusing to surrender them at gunpoint on April 9, 1940, or to compromise them afterwards. They were pillars that Henny and her extended family at the Royal Dockyards firmly embraced—none more so than *Gerda III*'s crew members.

Like most Danes, Henny faced the future with a combination of unwavering contempt for the Nazis, and a belief in Denmark's ability to endure and ultimately prevail. Inherently confident and unflappable, not even the Nazi invasion of Denmark seemed to unsettle the rhythm of her life.

In 1943, all of that changed. By August of that year, Denmark was becoming a battlefield between Nazi forces and a growing armed resistance movement. And, by the beginning of October, Hitler dispatched the Gestapo to round up Denmark's Jews and transport them to the concentration camps. These events brought the war to Henny's doorstep, and she threw herself into the battle— first as a leading participant in the Jewish rescue operation and then as a member of the armed resistance.

Henny's personal war against the Nazis lasted four turbulent months, ending only when she was forced to flee the country to save her own life.

Chapter Two

THE EARLY YEARS OF OCCUPATION

As Hitler's troops streamed across the border in unstoppable force, his chief envoy to Denmark, Cecil von Renthe-Fink, delivered a written ultimatum to Denmark's Foreign Minister Peter Munch. In keeping with the propaganda leaflets dropped over Copenhagen, the letter was laden with pretexts for the invasion, framed in terms of the purported need to protect Denmark from England and France. The "German military operations," the letter asserted, "were intended solely to secure" Denmark "against a planned occupation…by Anglo-French Armed Forces" that would deprive Denmark of its neutral status and convert it into a war zone.

Imbedded within the letter, and a similar letter delivered to Munch's counterpart in Norway, were acknowledgements of three of Germany's actual motives. These were the need to guard against "starvation" of the "German people" by preserving the flow of agricultural goods from Denmark; to safeguard "northern ore supplies" by securing their sources in Norway and their transportation routes through Danish waters; and to prevent a landing by "Anglo-French" forces that would enable them to attack Germany from a new northern flank.

Finally, the letter laid out the stark choice that confronted Denmark—resistance, which the letter made clear "would be broken by the deployed German forces...and lead only to bloodshed, completely to no avail," or the peaceful acceptance of German forces on Danish soil and territorial waters. So long as Denmark chose the latter path, the letter assured Munch, "Germany has no intention, now or in the future, of encroaching upon the Kingdom of Denmark's territorial integrity or political independence."

After the emergency meeting that ensued at Amalienborg Palace, Munch delivered Denmark's written response: Denmark would accept the occupation that was already a *fait accompli* under "the most serious protest"—and on the basis of the representation that its "territorial integrity" and "political independence" would be preserved.

The reciprocal statements that Denmark's "political independence" and "territorial integrity" would remain inviolate allowed a truce, and a period of icy coexistence, to take hold. Although the advantages of the truce were heavily weighted in Germany's favor, each side had something to show for it—and something to lose if Denmark descended into violence.

Germany achieved its objective of preserving, and over time expanding, its access to Danish ports, agriculture, and industry. It built and manned fortifications along Denmark's coastline, extending Germany's so-called "Atlantic Wall," to prevent the Allies from establishing a foothold on Germany's doorstep. Together with Germany's simultaneous conquest of Norway, it secured control over the entrance to the Baltic and established a secure route for transporting iron ore to German factories. And, by suppressing armed resistance before it could even begin, it did it all at minimal cost.

On the Danish side, the benefits of the agreement were measured not by gains, but by the avoidance of the devastating losses that the Nazis inflicted elsewhere. The agreement preserved Danish lives, averted the destruction of Denmark's cities, and avoided the imposition of martial law or a Nazi-imposed puppet regime. The Danish Parliament, for which elections continued to be held, was allowed to meet and enact laws that didn't interfere with the defensive activities of the occupation forces. Its Judiciary continued to apply Danish law and dispense justice on an impartial basis. Its civilian branches continued to serve the needs of the population in an orderly and just fashion. Even Denmark's military continued to exist at a reduced level—its naval vessels and crews confined to mine sweeping duties (clearing paths through floating mines that threatened coastal shipping), other life-saving operations, and police functions.

These basic elements of the agreement were clear. But room to differ about the meaning of "political independence" and "territorial integrity"—and the difficulty of reconciling those terms with having to accept a German occupation force against Denmark's will—made the letter exchange the start of a negotiating process rather than the end.

The ability of German troops to roam freely in Denmark made it clear that "territorial integrity" meant little beyond a promise not to annex Denmark or redraw the border between Germany and Denmark—no small thing in itself given what Germany had done elsewhere. The pledge of political independence, on the other hand, had enormous impact on the day-to-day lives of Denmark's Jews and other citizens. Leaders from across Denmark's political spectrum were united in the belief that political independence meant more than preserving Denmark's legislative, judicial, and other institutions. It also meant preserving individual rights—including the right of Danes to be treated equally regardless of their religion—that Denmark had long considered a bedrock of its political system.

With a mutual interest in averting, or at least deferring, violent confrontations, Denmark attempted to move forward under a so-called policy of cooperation. Under the terms of the cease fire, and the policy of cooperation that was meant to sustain it, Denmark retained substantial freedom for its people, while continuing to export food and manufactured goods to Germany and enabling German troops to man defensive positions on Denmark's coasts.

Attempting to live side-by-side with the Nazis was an experiment, thrust upon the Danes, that was doomed to fail. The diametrically opposed long-term goals of Nazi Germany and Denmark could be papered over for a time, but never reconciled. Denmark was intent on preserving a democratic government and a culture that were antithetical to everything the Nazis stood for. The Nazis were intent on chipping away at that democracy and gaining Danish acceptance of Nazi ideology one small step at a time.

In this, as in all else, the Nazis saw things through the lens of their racist ideology. If not entirely equal in Hitler's eyes to his mythical German "master race," Danes at least ranked close in his estimation. Hitler thus perceived the possibility that courting any Danes predisposed to his cause, rather than ruling with an iron fist from day one of the occupation, might enable a potent Nazi following to take root within Denmark. It was never more than a delusion. Beneath similarities that were literally only skin-deep, the Danes and their Nazi invaders were destined to remain implacable foes—hostile camps that time could only drive into greater conflict, not less.

During the long test of wills that inevitably followed the April 9 cease fire, disputes were initially confined to diplomatic channels. As part of the policy of cooperation, Denmark made some concessions (principally allowing a ban on political activities by Denmark's small Communist party) to keep the basic framework of the agreement intact. But Denmark also made clear that some matters were non-negotiable. Among these were its embrace of religious freedom, and its consequent refusal to allow the Nazis to impose anti-Semitic measures in Denmark—an objective the Nazis repeatedly thrust to the forefront of their agenda.

From the outset, the conflict between Nazi persecution of the Jews and Danish resolve to protect its Jewish population provided a test of which side was better served by the policy of cooperation, and of how long that policy could endure. For a time, the truce and the policy of cooperation served everyone's interests. But to Hitler and the Nazi zealots surrounding him, allowing the Danes to maintain the trappings of an independent state and allowing the

Jews to live somewhat normal lives—indeed allowing them to live at all—were never more than temporary expedients.

April 1940 through January 1942

After the initial trauma of the invasion subsided, an uneasy calm settled over Denmark.

The "political independence" that Denmark secured at the cease fire, and steadfastly preserved during the following years, allowed most facets of Danish life to continue unchanged. Even Denmark's nearly 8,350 Jews, protected by their government, continued their normal routines.[11] Jews in Denmark continued to live in their homes, practice their professions, and attend their synagogues, while the Nazis ruthlessly persecuted Jews throughout the rest of occupied Europe. But beneath this superficial adherence to routine, life for Danish Jews—beset by the unremitting stress of Nazi occupation—was far from normal. Hitler's anti-Semitic rants streamed over the air waves. Reports of the Nazis' persecution of Jews in Germany and its conquered territories reached Danish Jews through the press and from relatives and friends across the border. With Hitler's Berlin headquarters just 225 miles from Copenhagen, and his troops ever present on Denmark's streets, a dark cloud hung over Denmark's Jews. By the beginning of 1942, reports from Jews in other occupied countries were replaced by something even more ominous—silence—as the Nazis began the mass deportation of Jews to the death camps.

Denmark's initial ability to stop Nazi persecution of the Jews at the border—long after Nazi tanks and warplanes roared across it—rested in part on the written assurance of Denmark's "political independence." But these words would never have sufficed if Denmark's leaders and population had not made clear that the country was united on this issue, and that taking any action against Denmark's Jews would cause an uprising with severe consequences for Germany. Although Germany's military reigned supreme, an uprising within Denmark would wreak havoc on the supply of food and manufactured goods that the invasion was meant to secure, and require Germany to substantially increase its ground forces in Denmark by diverting troops that it needed elsewhere. German artillery and air power that were so effective in subduing weaker armed forces, could neither pound food from the ground nor goods from factories. They could only destroy the very resources that Germany wanted to exploit.

Cecil von Renthe-Fink, who continued to serve as Germany's senior representative in Denmark for two and one-half years after he delivered Hitler's April 9 ultimatum, was quick to advise Hitler's inner circle to leave Denmark's Jews alone. A career diplomat, Renthe-Fink favored the policy of cooperation. And, having been stationed in Denmark since 1936, he knew what demands would derail it. Six days after the start of the occupation, he sought to diffuse tensions by reporting to his foreign ministry that "the Danish authorities are apprehensive as to whether we will…take steps against the Jews," adding that "doing anything more in this respect than necessary…will cause paralysis of or serious disturbances in political and economic life." The severity of the repercussions, he concluded, "should not be underestimated."[12]

Despite that admonition, Nazi leaders in Berlin searched for signs of weakness on this issue within a matter of months. On September 18, 1940, King Christian X made a diary entry describing a conversation he held that day with Danish Prime Minister Thorvald Stauning. In light of recent German activity in other countries, the king stated his concern that the Nazis would at some point "demand the expulsion of Jews who were present" in Denmark—adding that any such demand "would definitely be repellant to me." Stauning responded that the Nazis had already raised "the question" in Berlin with the president of Denmark's National Bank, who told his Nazi hosts that he and other Danes would never tolerate such an action. Satisfied with that response, the king closed out the conversation by noting that "when we were determined the Germans backed off."[13]

Renthe-Fink again reiterated the need to maintain a hands-off policy with respect to Denmark's Jews on September 1, 1941, when

Hitler decreed that Jews "in the Greater German Reich" (Germany and the lands it had annexed) had to wear a yellow, fist-sized Star of David—the centuries-old symbol of the Jewish people—on their outer clothing. The yellow star edict was an element in the Nazis' methodical process of stigmatizing Jews and separating them, step-by-step, from the populations of which they had long been a part. It was intended to mark the Jews as a people unlike the rest of society, and unworthy of inclusion. It was another step the Danes would not tolerate. Correctly sensing the mood of the Danish people on this issue, Renthe-Fink reported that compelling Danish Jews to wear the yellow star "would arouse the protest of tens of thousands of Aryan Danes."[14] Although Jews were compelled to wear the yellow star throughout most of occupied Europe, the Jews in Denmark never did so.

Leni Yahil, an Israeli historian and author of a leading treatise on the rescue of the Danish Jews, wrote that Renthe-Fink "knew how to exploit the mentality of the Nazi leaders…to prevent or at least postpone an attack on the Jews of Denmark" but that "the decisive factor in the whole matter, as he himself maintained, was the firm stand of the Danish leaders, and people as one, on this question."[15]

The Danes' refusal to allow the Nazis to divide the population by compelling Jews to wear the yellow star gave rise to a popular myth. According to that myth, Denmark's King Christian X displayed solidarity with Denmark's Jews by wearing a yellow Star of David during his daily horseback rides through Copenhagen. Although mythical, the story is rooted in fact. Its origin lies in a heartfelt remark that the king made in September 1941 to Vilhelm Buhl, Denmark's finance minister and acting prime minister. As the king recorded in his diary, Buhl expressed concern that Hitler would extend his star edict to Denmark. Both men agreed that, if the Nazis made such a demand upon the Danish government, they "would have to reject it outright under the constitution." The king then added that, if the Nazis bypassed the Danish government, and directly ordered Danish Jews to wear the yellow star, "the right thing would be for all of us to wear it."[16]

Buhl made no secret of the king's remarks, making the conversation widely enough known to come to the attention of a Norwegian political cartoonist, Ragnvald Blix. Blix had attracted fame—as well as Hitler's wrath—for a long series of anti-fascist cartoons that he drew for Norwegian, Danish, and Swedish newspapers before Hitler invaded Denmark and Norway. Following the invasions, Blix went into exile in Sweden where his works— deemed too incendiary by the Danish and Norwegian press in the post-invasion period—continued to appear in Sweden's most stridently anti-Nazi newspaper. On January 10, 1942, four months after the conversation between the king and Buhl took place, that newspaper ran Blix's caricature of the two men deep in thought—a caricature that showed the king clad in the riding boots and uniform that he wore on his daily horseback rides. A caption, hewing close to the facts, paraphrased the content of their conversation about how to respond if the Nazis required the Jews of Denmark to wear the yellow star. The illustration and its caption caught the imagination of the world, leading to retellings in which the king not only stated his intention to wear the Star of David *if* Danish Jews were compelled to do so, but actually wore it in a show of solidarity.[17]

King Christian X demonstrated his solidarity with Denmark's Jews in other notable ways, but he never wore a yellow Star of David for the simple reason that his Jewish subjects never had to do so. It is a rare instance in which the truth is better than the myth, and it perfectly illustrates how the Danes prevented the Nazis from getting their program for instilling anti-Semitism off the ground in Denmark. Aside from the specter of mass protests predicted by Renthe-Fink, and possibly of a more forceful uprising, the Danes made it known that they would upend the edict—rendering it not merely pointless but counterproductive—by converting the Nazis' symbol of division into a symbol of national unity. The king's readiness to lead all Danes in wearing the Jewish star if any Dane were forced to do so applied a broader principle—that nations thrive when their people support one another as fellow countrymen, and rot when they divide along religious or ethnic lines. Danish leaders reiterated and reinforced that principle in speeches, newspaper columns, and open letters throughout the years of Nazi occupation. The primacy of the Danes' shared status as countrymen, and their obligation to defend fellow countrymen who came under attack, was a bedrock foundation of Danish society that most Danes fully appreciated.

Exempting Danish Jews from the yellow star edict marked another victory in Denmark's continuing effort to prevent the Nazis from driving a wedge between Denmark's Christians and Jews. It was something in which all Danes could take satisfaction.

The ground, however, had already shifted in ways that would soon make the battle more difficult and more desperate. On July 31, 1941, one month before Nazis put the yellow star edict into effect in Germany and the lands it had annexed, Hitler's top deputy Hermann Göring ordered his staff to draw up plans for the "final solution to the Jewish problem in Europe"—the Nazi term for killing all of Europe's Jews.

The groundwork for murdering millions of Jews—the years-long process of converting the unthinkable to the seemingly inevitable— began by separating and degrading them. Hitler started the process in Germany in 1933, the year he rose to power, by enacting legislation that excluded Jews from government service, drove most Jewish students out of German universities and public schools, and revoked the citizenship of naturalized Jews. In the following years, Germany enacted laws (beginning with what became known as the Nuremberg Laws) that barred Jews from marrying Christians, excluded Jews from the legal profession, made it illegal for Jewish doctors to treat non-Jewish patients, and deprived all German Jews of their citizenship. (Had the same restriction been placed on Jewish doctors in Denmark, King Christian X would have had to find a replacement for his Jewish physician.) Laws enacted and decrees issued in Nazi Germany in 1938 barred the few remaining Jewish students from public schools and universities, and forced the closure or transfer of Jewish owned businesses. Jews whose names were of "non-Jewish" origin were compelled to adopt new names—"Israel" for men and "Sara" for women—to further set them apart. The 1941 order compelling Jews to wear the yellow Star of David was another step—the last step—before they could be removed altogether.

In November 1941, with plans for the "final solution" nearing completion, Hitler's deputies began to pressure Denmark to enact "Jewish legislation" patterned on the laws adopted by Germany. Nazi demands and Danish refusals first took place behind the scenes, in conferences between government ministers, but soon became matters of public discussion.

Denmark's foreign minister, Erik Scavenius, met with Göring in Berlin on November 25, 1941. Pressing Scavenius to follow Germany's lead, Göring told him that Denmark could no longer "circumvent the Jewish problem." To this, Scavenius reported to his prime minister, "I replied as always that there was no Jewish problem in Denmark." Upon his return to Copenhagen, Scavenius gave a second report about his exchange with Göring to the Unity Council. In the summer of 1940, Parliament created this nine-person Council, composed of leaders of Denmark's five major political parties, to assure that Parliament could act quickly, and with a single voice, on matters concerning the Nazis. To a man, the Unity Council concluded that "developments of this sort should be halted at the first moment" and that Denmark could never permit the "introduction of Jewish legislation."[18]

As word of these demands spread, and fears grew within the Jewish community, Denmark's minister of religious affairs invited the chief rabbi of Copenhagen's century-old Great Synagogue to meet with him. Speaking on behalf of the government, the minister assured him that no anti-Jewish legislation would be tolerated in Denmark and that "as long as a Danish government has anything to say in this country, the Jews have no grounds for fear."[19]

The Danish people, their elected leaders, and their king remained united on this issue. As the Danes saw it, preserving the equality guaranteed to Jews under Danish law was an essential part of preserving Danish self-rule. If they could no longer keep Danish Jews free within their own country—where religious freedom had long been a basic tenet of Danish society—Danes could no longer cling to any illusions about their own freedom and independence.

One of the most eloquent proponents of that view was Hal Koch, a popular young theologian and Professor of Church History at Copenhagen University. In the months following the invasion, Koch embarked on a mission to inspire his fellow Danes to actively defend their democratic principles against assault by foreign forces and anyone seeking to erode them from within. To that end, Koch commenced a ten-part lecture series, on September 18, 1940, that catapulted him to national prominence.

Evoking a past in which Danes rebounded from military defeats and prolonged crises by standing "at each other's sides" and "laying stone upon stone," Koch called upon every Dane to play their part. "Let us remember," he said, that "the future of Denmark" must be "built up in and by each one of us" and that "every time one of us fails, there is an empty place in the line." We must, he said, "walk the road together." A realist, Koch told his audiences that the road would be a long one. "We cannot gain from the past a belief that everything will soon be again as it was, for there is no ground to believe that what we are faced with is a temporary storm."[20]

Koch's lectures, given at Copenhagen University but open to the public, drew overflow crowds and were printed in full in the Danish press. In November 1940, he was named chairman of the Union of Danish Youth and, in that capacity, gave speeches in nearly every Danish town and village. As one scholarly analysis of his work put it, Koch spoke "not only to students and professors, but to farmers, factory workers, clerks and fishermen."[21] His speeches also caught the attention of the Nazis, who attempted to assassinate him by planting a bomb in his home in June 1942, and incarcerated him in August 1943.

In January 1942, with Nazi demands to impose anti-Jewish measures in Denmark becoming more strident, Koch tackled the subject head-on in a column that was published in a leading Copenhagen newspaper. He began that column by asserting that imposing "an active anti-Jewish policy" on Denmark would "trample on" the promise of "political independence" that Germany made to Denmark in April 1940 to bring about the truce. Embracing a widely shared belief, his premise was that "political independence" meant nothing if Nazi Germany could divide the Danish population in ways that Denmark abhorred, and command the Danish government to deprive any segment of its population of political rights and personal freedoms that had long been the birthright of all Danes. It wasn't only the Jews who were in danger, it was Danish democracy itself. In Koch's words:

> Certainly, this is a question of right and justice for the Jews, but in addition—and this is something fundamental— justice and freedom in Danish life is at stake. We should not forget that our country's fate will be decided not by the war in the outside world but by the extent to which we are able to maintain truth, justice and freedom by being ready to pay the price.[22]

These statements and others like them were no doubt reassuring to Danish Jews, but the fact that the issue had to be addressed at all signaled the arrival of a more dangerous phase. What the Danish Jews and their countrymen could not yet fully comprehend was that the Nazis' more strident calls to address the "Jewish problem" were propelled by the looming implementation of the "Final Solution."

The same month that Koch published his article on "justice and freedom" in the Danish press, fifteen high ranking Nazi leaders met at a lakeside mansion in the Berlin suburb of Wansee to complete their plan to annihilate Europe's Jews. The "Final Solution" that Göring ordered his subordinates to draw up in July was now being put into operation.

January 1942 through August 1943

SS General Reinhard Heydrich presided over the January 20, 1942 Wansee Conference, accompanied by SS Lieutenant Colonel

Adolf Eichman and other SS Officers. The issue before them was not whether to implement the plan—that decision had already been made by Hitler and his top aides—but how to do so most thoroughly and efficiently. The decisions made at that meeting were recorded in a document known as the Wansee Protocol. That document stated that "Europe is to be combed through from West to East" to implement "the Final Solution." Jews were to be transported first to "transit ghettos" and then "further east from there" to the death camps. A representative from Hitler's Foreign Office predicted that there would be "no great difficulty [in] the southeast and west of Europe" but that the certainty of "difficulties" in Denmark and other "Nordic countries" made it "advisable to postpone action in these countries for the present." The threat of a Danish uprising bought time for the Jews within its borders, but granting a "postponement…for the present" meant that they were not to be spared in the end.[23]

The Wansee Protocol also made clear that the few Jews who might still have been able to escape Nazi territory were now trapped. If the "Final Solution" were to live up to its name—and the Nazis firmly resolved that it would—merely forcing Jews to leave European soil would no longer suffice. Jews throughout Europe had to be captured and killed, leaving no possibility of an eventual return. The Protocol thus stated that Hitler has now "forbidden the emigration of Jews." The prior "emigration" policy, which effectively ground to a halt at the start of the war, "has been replaced by deportation of the Jews to the East," where gas chambers would be their ultimate destination.[24]

Results of the Wansee Conference soon became plain to see throughout occupied Europe, even if the end result was still obscured. In March 1942, the Nazis began the mass deportation of Jews from France; in July 1942, they began to deport Jews from the Netherlands; in August 1942, the Nazis began to deport Jews from Belgium. All over Europe, Jews were rapidly disappearing and being transported to "the East." In Denmark, newspaper accounts conveyed the overall horror of the deportations while individual loss was often measured by silence—by letters that went unanswered and cards that no longer came.

The Jews in Denmark were living on borrowed time. The slender thread on which their lives depended—the continued ability of the Danish government to shelter them from persecution—could be broken by Nazi force at any moment.

As Jews across the rest of Europe were rounded up and sent to their deaths, the Nazi high command ordered Renthe-Fink to force concessions from the Danes. It was one thing for Denmark to resist anti-Semitic measures while Jews were simply being isolated and degraded throughout the rest of occupied Europe. It was another thing for Denmark to undermine the "Final Solution"—now that Hitler's ultimate goal seemed within his grasp—by resolutely preserving the dignity and the lives of the Jews with its borders.

Renthe-Fink met with Scavenius on August 24, 1942, in what Renthe-Fink described as the hope of "heading off the storm" by "getting the Danes to keep Jewish influence in public life under control." Scavenius described the meetings in even darker terms, reporting that Renthe-Fink "was much more aggressive" than in the past and had demanded the "removal of Jews from all key positions." Once again, Scavenius' reply was swift and firm: the Danes "would regard this as a denial of their own ideals" and "would not act against their own citizens."[25] The period of cooperation and diplomacy was reaching its inevitable end.

On September 29, 1942, Hitler removed Renthe-Fink from his post in Denmark and replaced him with Werner Best. Best was a Nazi ideologue, a co-founder of the Gestapo, and a high-ranking member of the dreaded SS—the group that Hitler formed to ruthlessly eliminate dissent and enforce his murderous edicts throughout Nazi-controlled territory. Only the terms of Germany's truce with Denmark constrained Best's power in that country, at least for the moment. Best's arrival in Copenhagen on November 5, clad in the uniform of an SS *Obergrupenfürer*, signaled the start of a more confrontational era. Israeli historian Leni Yahil summed up Renthe-Fink as a traditional diplomat "who was Hitler's official representative yet no anti-Semite, who supported the occupation of Denmark by the Reich but did not wish to force National Socialism on the Danes...."[26] Werner Best, a strident ant-Semite and ardent Nazi, presented neither of these contradictions.

Hitler also sent a new military commander, General Hermann von Hanneken, to take command of German forces in Denmark. His arrival coincided with a massive escalation of Germany's military presence that was intended both to repel a feared Allied invasion of the Danish coast—a coast at Germany's doorstep—and to stamp out any domestic threat to Nazi interests. Within a year of von Hanneken's arrival, the number of Nazi troops in Denmark soared from 20,000 to 150,000.

These changes, coupled with news from the rest of Europe, put Danish Jews—and the nation as a whole—under even greater stress. The mass deportation of Jews to "the East" had been known for some time. By the end of 1942, rumors reached Denmark about what awaited the deported Jews in the East—rumors that the Nazis were engaging in mass murder.[27]

The executive committee of Denmark's Jewish Community gathered at the beginning of 1943 to discuss whether the time had come to make preparations to hide within Denmark or escape to unoccupied Sweden. The committee decided against any action. For some, faith in the Danish government's ability to protect them, and fear that discovery of an escape plan might undermine the government's authority or provoke Nazi retaliation, was reason enough to do nothing. For everyone at the meeting, it seemed that no viable alternative existed. As Yahil described it, "the members of the committee were all agreed that...it was impossible to hide six or seven thousand Jews without the help of the non-Jewish inhabitants of the country" and that it was impossible to make "such a request or expect that it would be met." They further agreed that "it did not seem likely...that very many could escape to Sweden."[28]

The members of the executive committee had good reason to doubt the feasibility of escaping to Sweden. It had already been tried, on a small scale, with dire consequences. Soon after the Nazis invaded Denmark, a few fishermen set out across the Øresund with Jews hidden in their boats. Although the trip to Sweden was successful, the fisherman—in a precursor of what was to befall some rescuers in 1943—were arrested by the Nazis when they returned to their home ports.[29] German naval patrols that were visible from shore, and the very real risk of hitting an unseen mine, added to the sense that a maritime evacuation would be nearly impossible. It was a view that prevailed until there was no alternative—and then weighed heavily on the refugees and rescuers who ultimately put it to the test.

AS 1943 WORE ON, it became a year of increasing confrontation. With Germany tightening its grip, and Danes growing weary of the occupation, the period of uneasy coexistence turned toward active resistance and brutal suppression. In the summer of 1943, acts of sabotage, strikes, and reprisals began to spread across Denmark. Nazi occupation forces and the emerging Danish resistance movement were on a collision course. In August 1943, they collided head on.

On August 25, workers at Copenhagen's Forum, the largest exhibition hall in Scandinavia, were completing its conversion into barracks for another 2,000 German troops who were scheduled to arrive the following day. At lunchtime, a delivery boy pedaled into the building, a Tuborg Beer carton strapped to his bicycle. His path had been cleared by five men, all members of a resistance group called Holger Danske, who had taken the guards away at gunpoint and emptied the building of workers. Three members of Holger Danske then stood watch outside the Forum while the group's two leaders entered the building. Inside, they carefully unpacked the Tuborg carton, placed its actual contents—more than 100 pounds of explosives—at the base of the building's support columns, attached fuses, and raced to the exit. Just as they reached the street, running full tilt, explosions reduced the building to a pile of rubble that remained unusable for the next twelve years.[30]

Chapter Three

THE END OF THE TRUCE

THE EXPLOSION AT THE FORUM, and the Nazi demands that followed it, shattered what little remained of any working relationship between the Nazi occupation authorities and Denmark's leaders. On Saturday, August 28, 1943, Werner Best delivered an ultimatum to the Danish government. To remain in power, it would have to turn on its own people. Anti-Nazi voices would have to be silenced. Death sentences would have to be imposed on Danish saboteurs.

The ultimatum required little discussion. Before the day was over, the government—elected officials and King Christian X—rejected the Nazis' demands completely. The decision was a foregone conclusion, and the Nazis were prepared for it.

In a proclamation that went into effect on Sunday morning, the Nazis declared a state of emergency and imposed martial law. Parliament was disbanded and would not meet again until the war was over. Gatherings of more than five persons were prohibited in both public and private spaces, a sunset curfew was imposed, firearms and explosives were confiscated, press censorship was imposed, strikes were banned, civil servants were compelled to obey newly installed Nazi supervisors, mail and telephone service were temporarily halted, and special tribunals were established to sentence resisters. To further compel obedience, German troops were posted outside all government facilities, and hundreds of prominent Danes were taken into custody. Military bases that had remained in Danish hands were overrun by Nazi forces. Any semblance of Danish autonomy was brought to a sudden, and sometimes violent, end.

The most violent confrontation that Sunday morning took place at the Royal Dockyards, the centuries-old homeport of the Danish navy. What transpired there contributed to the success of the flotilla that carried the Jews to safety one month later.

Denmark had been allowed to keep most of its naval fleet— apart from six torpedo boats that the Nazis confiscated in 1941—to carry out training, life-saving, and mine sweeping operations.[31] The imposition of martial law brought that to an end. At 4:00 a.m. on August 29, German troops stormed the Royal Dockyards, seeking to take over the base and the warships that were stationed there. Denmark's Rear Admiral A.H. Vedel had already ordered his officers not to surrender any vessel to the Nazis. Under his standing orders, warships that could escape to Sweden were directed to do so. Warships that could not escape were to be blown up at their docks. From 4:13 to 4:35 a.m., Danish defenders used small arms and grenades to hold off German troops while explosive charges ripped the fleet apart. The explosions rattled windows across the harbor in Copenhagen and south of the Dockyards in Christianshavn. They reverberated in Henny's Christianshavn home, shaking her world in more ways than one.

When the explosions ended, twenty-nine warships were ablaze or on the bottom. Among them was the *Peder Skram* (a 286-foot "coastal defense" vessel that was essentially a small scale battle ship), four torpedo boats, ten submarines, and twelve minesweepers and mine layers. Only six operational vessels fell into German hands.

The Danish warships that attempted to escape to Sweden had limited success. Thirteen vessels—a patrol boat, three minesweepers, and nine other small vessels—reached Sweden and were confined to Swedish ports for the rest of the war. Other vessels that tried to escape never made it.

Denmark's second coastal defense ship, the 295-foot *Niels Iuel*, was anchored in a fjord north of Copenhagen when the naval base was attacked. Its attempt to escape to Sweden was cut short when the ship was intercepted and attacked by the Luftwaffe, Germany's air force. After four bombing and strafing runs, the ship's captain ordered the crew to run the ship aground and destroy its engines and weapons before it could be boarded.

The 223-foot patrol boat *Hvidbjørnen* ("*Polar Bear*") was also intercepted by a German warship as it sought to make its escape. The crew scuttled the ship with explosives before it could be captured. Among the cadets on board was Sven Kieler, who would soon join forces with Henny and whose fight against the Nazis was just beginning.

The personnel who defended the base and manned the vessels were taken prisoner and interned at the Royal Dockyards. The original internees were subsequently joined by another cadet, Eric Koch Michaelsen, known to his friends as "Mix," who was destined to play a significant role in the rescue of the Danish Jews, in the Danish resistance, and in Henny's life.

MIX WAS AT HOME in a Copenhagen neighborhood somewhat distant from the harbor, nearing the end of a month-long leave, when the Nazis stormed the navy base. When word of the attack reached him that Sunday morning, Mix reacted in a way that revealed much about his character: he donned his uniform, got on his bicycle, and rode toward the battle—not realizing that it was already over. As Mix neared the Royal Dockyards a civilian warned him off, telling him what had taken place at the base and reporting that the Nazis were on the hunt for any military personal not yet in custody. The danger was quickly confirmed when Mix saw two Danish soldiers being marched off under Nazi guard, and then heard a gunshot and a shouted order to halt. Mix didn't wait around to find out who the shot and order were aimed at. He sped down a side street where he took off his navy cap and jacket, put on a civilian jacket that a helpful young man handed to him, and then rode off, already formulating a plan to rejoin the Danish warships that had escaped to Sweden.

Hours later, Mix reached his family's waterfront summer home at Solrød Strand, nineteen miles southwest of Copenhagen, where he kept a sailing kayak. As soon as he arrived, he went to work rigging the boat and painting a blue camouflage pattern over its white hull and sail. He then waited until darkness to set sail across twenty-five miles of open sea to the southwestern tip of Sweden.

Mix began his passage at ten o'clock on Sunday night, in a favorable wind under a crescent moon. He expected to reach Sweden, near the fishing village of Skanor, by six or seven o'clock in the morning. For hours he made good speed, sailing east-southeast toward his destination, and his spirits ran high. His camouflage paint gave him confidence, but not overconfidence. As he crossed the waters south of Copenhagen, he repeatedly hauled in his sail and made quick turns toward the Danish coast to present a smaller target to the German searchlights that swept over him every fifteen minutes. By four o'clock in the morning, he had covered nearly twenty miles and was beyond the range of the Nazis' coastal lights and fortifications. The Drogden Lighthouse, which provided a helpful bearing, was off his port side five miles to the north. The rotating beacon atop the Falsterbro Lighthouse, marking his destination on the Swedish shore, was in sight directly ahead, just over five miles away. But he would get no closer to Sweden than that.

Shortly after four o'clock in the morning, there was a sudden change in the weather. Mix found himself in an "ugly blow," as he described it, that overpowered his boat and obscured his view of the coast. To stave off disaster, Mix lashed the sail and boom to his mast. He then began paddling into the wind and wind-driven waves that were pushing him further from his destination, waves that could easily capsize his boat if it turned broadside to the building seas. As the winds continued to build, Mix's mast snapped off at its base, leaving a tangled mass of spars and canvas dragging in the water alongside the boat. Mix crawled on his stomach over the narrow foredeck to cut the debris away before it could puncture the hull or pull it under. Back in the cockpit, with that task done, he resumed paddling into the oncoming waves. With no land in sight, and no compass to guide him, Mix merely tried to hold his position, hoping that conditions would improve and that he could regain his bearings by sunrise. But, by the time the sun rose at six that morning, an impenetrable fog had enveloped him. By seven o'clock, with his energy spent and his position still unknown, Mix drifted off figuratively as well as literally.

Mix awoke at half past nine, exhausted and cold, in a half-submerged boat. The wind had abated, but the thick fog that rolled in kept any land well out of sight. All Mix could make out was a German minesweeper about one mile to his side, and what appeared to be the stack of a steamship dead ahead and pointing toward him. Mix summoned a final burst of energy and paddled in its direction. As he closed the gap, it proved to be no ship at all. Instead, the Drogden Lighthouse, standing tall atop its man-made island, slowly came into view. Just one month earlier, the German occupation forces had whitewashed the Lighthouse, covering its usually distinctive red stripes to make it less of a landmark for Allied aviators and mariners. On this day, the lighthouse was rendered even paler and less recognizable by the fog.

Mix reached a landing at the base of the lighthouse and began climbing a staircase that led to the top of its pedestal, hoping to find that Danish lighthouse keepers were the sole occupants. But, as he continued to ascend, the green uniforms on personnel atop the pedestal told him otherwise. By the time Mix reached the lighthouse on August 30, 1943, German forces had converted it into a military observation post, fortified with an anti-aircraft cannon and other weapons. In addition to its usual keepers, the lighthouse was manned by German soldiers who captured Mix and demolished the craft that brought him to them. Mix was then held prisoner at the lighthouse for eight days before a Nazi patrol boat brought him back to the Royal Dockyards to be interned with the officers and cadets who were already held there.

The eight days that Mix spent at the lighthouse were not as unpleasant as one might expect. With his boat sunk, the lighthouse as a whole became an inescapable prison. There was therefore no need, and apparently no desire, to confine him any further. The Danish lighthouse crew, Mix reported, treated him like royalty, while the German troops seemed to find him an interesting diversion. Free to roam within the confined space of the lighthouse and its pedestal, Mix observed the daily arrivals of *Gerda III* and met its crew during their visits—encounters that proved consequential for Mix, for Henny, and for the Jews that *Gerda III* later saved.[32]

Chapter Four

THE WAR AGAINST THE JEWS REACHES DENMARK

By THE TIME MARTIAL LAW was imposed in Denmark, Hitler's campaign to exterminate Europe's Jews had been underway for more than two years. In Ukraine and other Soviet territory, roving death squads (the Einsatzgruppen) rounded up Jews and gunned them down by the tens of thousands soon after Nazi forces invaded the Soviet Union in June 1941. In December 1941, poison gas vans went into operation at Chelmo, the Nazis' first death camp. In February 1942, the Nazis put gas chambers and crematoriums into operation at Auschwitz. By the summer of 1943, the Nazis were murdering thousands of Jews per day at Auschwitz alone, while rapidly building its killing capacity to as many as 6,000 people per day. They were committing similar atrocities, on a somewhat smaller scale, at five other death camps. Now, with the August 29 martial law decree in place, and Nazi forces exercising direct control over Denmark's internal affairs, the Nazis decided that the time had come to "solve the Jewish problem" in Denmark.

During these years of carnage, the Nazis refrained from attacking Jews within Denmark for a purely practical reason: the Danes had made clear that persecuting their Jewish countrymen would trigger a nationwide revolt. But, as the "Final Solution"

31

gained momentum across the rest of Europe, Hitler's obsession with annihilating the Jews overrode such considerations. With the rise of the Danish resistance, moreover, the feared revolt had already begun. That it could get much worse no longer seemed to matter. And so, the Nazis hatched a plan to round up Denmark's Jews and transport them to the Theresienstadt concentration camp in occupied Czechoslovakia—a place that for most arrivals was a temporary stopover on the way to the Auschwitz and Treblinka death camps.

On September 8, 1943, Werner Best telegraphed the Nazi leadership in Berlin that the state of emergency afforded him the opportunity he needed. He wrote (in language that underestimated Denmark's Jewish population):

> I hereby beg, in light of the new situation, to report on the Jewish problem in Denmark as follows: In accordance with the consistent application of the new policy in Denmark, it is my opinion that measures should now be taken toward a solution of the problem of the Jews.... In order to arrest and deport some 6,000 Jews (including women and children) at one sweep it is necessary to have the police forces I requested in my telegram...of 9/1. Almost all of them should be put to work in greater Copenhagen where the majority of the local Jews live. Supplemental forces should be provided by the German military commander in Denmark. For transportation, ships must be considered a prime necessity and should be ordered in time....[33]

A few days later, Hitler's foreign minister Ribbentrop (later sentenced to death at the Nuremberg war crime trials) asked Best to "put forward concrete proposals with regard to the deportation of the Jews," including the number of SS troops that "should be detailed to the implementation of the operation in question."[34]

On September 11, Best delivered the plan to Ribbentrop, who passed it on to Hitler. The plan called for two German transport ships to arrive in Copenhagen on Rosh Hashanah—the start of the Jewish New Year and High Holy Days. With the ships in place, truckloads of Gestapo forces would fan out to conduct midnight raids on Jewish homes throughout Copenhagen and the surrounding area. They would be guided by membership lists that the Nazis stole by breaking into and ransacking the offices of the Jewish Community of Denmark, an organization to which many Jews throughout Denmark belonged. As the raids progressed, and after they concluded, the Gestapo would take the captured Jews to the waiting ships to begin their journey to Theresienstadt. Other Nazi forces would simultaneously scour the rest of the country, capturing Jews wherever they might reside. Hitler ordered his staff to give Best all of the troops, transport ships, and other equipment that he needed to carry out the plan.[35]

On September 18, Adolph Eichmann, the SS officer in charge of transporting Jews from all corners of occupied Europe to the death camps, sent a Gestapo contingent to Copenhagen under the command of Colonel Rudolph Mildner. Before he was transferred to Denmark, Mildner was the Gestapo chief in Katowice, Poland, and was responsible for sending thousands of Polish Jews to their death at Auschwitz. The plan to eradicate Denmark's Jews was now in motion.

The next day, Best disclosed the plan to Georg Ferdinand Duckwitz, a civilian member of the German occupation staff who was responsible for commercial port operations in Copenhagen. That disclosure would have vast unintended consequences. Duckwitz had already attempted to dissuade Best and the Nazi command in Berlin from subjecting Denmark's Jews to the "Final Solution." Now any chance of changing the outcome by working within the chain of command was over. The only options that remained for Duckwitz were to accept the decision or go down the perilous path of subverting it. Duckwitz wrote in his diary on September 19, "I know what I have to do." His chosen course of action would take him on a secret mission to Sweden, to a clandestine meeting with Danish political leaders, and to a German naval officer who commanded the German patrol boats based in Copenhagen.[36]

On September 21, Duckwitz flew to Sweden to inform Prime Minister Hansson about the Nazis' plan, and to ask him to provide refuge for Denmark's Jews. After an emergency meeting with his cabinet, Hansson told Duckwitz that Sweden would only allow the Danish Jews to enter Sweden if the Nazi leadership in Berlin approved. Hansson stated that he sent a telegram to Berlin and would inform Duckwitz of Berlin's reply. Not surprisingly there was no reply and no change in the Nazi plan. More would have to be done, and Duckwitz was prepared to do it. He wrote in his diary on September 27 that "there will be no detour from the road I have taken."[37]

On September 28, Best told Duckwitz that the last detail, the timing of the raids, had been decided. Denmark's Jews would be rounded up and deported during the night of Friday, October 1 and the early morning hours of Saturday, October 2. They would be trapped in their homes while they were gathered for both the Sabbath and the High Holy Days—the ten-day period from Rosh Hashanah (the Jewish New Year) to Yom Kippur (the Day of Atonement).

That afternoon, Duckwitz met with leaders of Denmark's Social Democrats, the country's longtime ruling party, to set a rescue in motion. Hans Hedtoft, the chairman of the party (and Denmark's two-time prime minister after the war) recalled that Duckwitz entered the "worker's old meeting place," where Hedtoft and his associates were gathered, and laid out exactly what was about to happen:

> Now the disaster is about to occur.... The whole thing is planned in full detail. Ships are going to anchor in the harbor of Copenhagen. Your poor Jewish fellow countrymen who will be found by the Gestapo will be forcibly transported to the ships and deported to an unknown fate.[38]

Hedtoft, in his own words, "became speechless with rage and anxiety," and just managed to say, "thank you for the news" before Duckwitz "disappeared."

Hedtoft and other party leaders raced to begin the warning process and to offer their help. Hedtoft took it upon himself to visit the home of Carl Bernard Henriques, the Chairman of Copenhagen's Jewish Community and a prominent attorney known for his advocacy in Denmark's Supreme Court. Henriques, whose family had lived in Denmark for more than three centuries, proved difficult to convince that it was suddenly necessary to flee. With his false sense of security, he would not be the appropriate messenger. Later that night, another emissary from Hedtoft's party met with Marcus Melchior, the acting chief rabbi of Copenhagen's Great Synagogue. At this point, less than seventy-two hours remained to inform Denmark's Jews of the need to escape their homes and businesses, and to help them secure temporary hiding places.

The next morning, September 29, about one hundred members of the Great Synagogue gathered for a service preceding that evening's start of Rosh Hashanah. Instead of the customary service, Rabbi Melchior gave them a dire warning and a stark set of instructions.

> Last night I received word that the Germans plan to raid Jewish homes throughout Copenhagen to arrest all the Danish Jews for shipment to concentration camps.... We must take action immediately. You must leave the Synagogue now and contact all relatives, friends and neighbors you know are Jewish and tell them what I have told you. You must tell them to pass the word on to everyone they know is Jewish. You must also speak to all your Christian friends and tell them to warn the Jews. You must do this immediately, within the next few minutes, so that two or three hours from now everyone will know what is happening. By...tonight we must all be in hiding.[39]

After warning his congregation, Rabbi Melchior called a friend, the minister of a Lutheran church sixty miles from Copenhagen. The minister readily agreed to hide Rabbi Melchior, the rabbi's wife, and their five children in the minister's own home. Rabbi Melchior then asked the minister of the Trinitatas Lutheran Church, down the street from the synagogue, to hide the synagogue's torahs and other holy objects. The minister readily agreed.

Over ninety-five percent of Denmark's Jewish population lived in Copenhagen, making it easier to spread the word. Warnings fanned out from political and religious leaders. Teachers warned students. Employers and union leaders warned their employees and members. Friends called on friends. Some Danes warned strangers who they thought might be Jewish. An ambulance driver made rounds to Jewish homes, guided only by what appeared to be Jewish names in a telephone directory that he yanked from a phone booth. Through the spontaneous efforts of Jews and non-Jews alike, almost all of Denmark's Jews were alerted within a matter of hours to the danger that confronted them. And so, by the night of September 29, when Jews would normally be preparing to usher in the New Year, Denmark's Jews were preparing to go underground or had already done so. By the next day, Rosh Hashanah morning, the synagogue was closed.

Late on the night of October 1, trucks filled with Gestapo agents left their staging grounds according to plan. By 10:00 p.m., they had cordoned off escape routes and began their sweep. Using the names and addresses that the Nazis had stolen from the Jewish Community offices weeks earlier, they sped through the streets to Jewish homes—and found nearly all of them empty.

Only 202 Danish Jews, almost all of whom had been living in a home for the elderly, were captured that night in Copenhagen and taken away by ship. Another eighty-two Jews were captured on Denmark's Jutland Peninsula and taken away in railroad freight cars.[40] Approximately 8,060 Jews had escaped the trap—at least for the moment.

On October 2, Werner Best issued a proclamation that was either written before the raids or carefully worded to obscure the result. In a misguided attempt to placate the Danes and turn them against the Jews, Best wrote:

> [I]n consideration of the fact that the Jews, who by their anti-German propaganda activity and their...support of terror and sabotage actions...have contributed to the deterioration of the situation in Denmark, have been removed from public life by the measures taken from the German side, and have been prevented from continuing to poison the atmosphere, and in fulfillment of the desire entertained in wide circles of the Danish population, the release of the interned soldiers [and sailors] will begin in the next few days....

In Denmark, Best's attempt to blame the Jews for the growing hostility between the Danes and the Nazi invaders who occupied their country was universally rejected. His boast about driving Danish Jews "from public life"—an act most Danes considered an intolerable attack on fellow countrymen—merely added fuel to the fire. And in Berlin, the notion that the Jews had been "removed from public life" did not disguise the fact that they had not been captured and shipped off to a concentration camp. When the results reached them on October 2, Hitler and SS Commander Heinrich Himmler were furious. Himmler sent Eichmann to Denmark on Sunday, October 3, to rectify the situation. Upon his arrival, Eichmann ordered Mildner—who needed little encouragement in any case—to find the Jews at all costs. It was impossible, Eichmann insisted, for the Danish Jews to remain in hiding for more than a few days.

As Eichmann was rousing the Gestapo, other powerful voices were rousing the Danes.

On the Sunday that Eichmann arrived in Denmark, a letter that the Bishop of Copenhagen wrote on behalf of all the bishops of the Danish Lutheran Church, to which ninety percent of Danes belonged, was read in churches throughout the country. The letter began by declaring that "whenever Jews are persecuted for racial or religious reasons, it is the duty of the Christian Church to protest against such persecution"—and it built from there. It explicitly drew upon "the understanding of justice" that is "rooted in the Danish people," that was "settled through centuries in our Danish Christian culture," and that is enshrined "in our constitution." These bedrocks of Danish society, the bishops declared, establish that "all Danish citizens have...freedom of religion, and a right to worship God in accordance with their own vocation and conscience...so that race or religion can never in itself become the cause of deprivation of anybody's rights, freedom or property." Therefore, the letter concluded, we must "fight to preserve for our Jewish brothers and sisters the same freedom which we ourselves value more than life itself."[41]

Similar calls came from other quarters. The Freedom Council, a group that had been formed by resistance leaders in mid-September, issued a proclamation through the underground press that "call[ed] on the Danish population to help in every way possible those Jewish fellow citizens who have not yet succeeded in escaping abroad." It also warned that "every Dane who renders help to the Germans in their persecution of human beings is a traitor and will be punished as such when Germany is defeated."[42]

The situation in Denmark on October 4 was summed up in a *New York Times* dispatch from Stockholm:

> Danish patriots blasted German troop barracks, two power stations and two war material factories in a reintensified sabotage campaign today that provided a military answer to Germany's attempted purge of the Jews in Denmark.... Danish soldiers who have been released from the internment in which they had been held since...August 29, have refused to sign statements pledging themselves not to aid opposition groups. The Germans had sought to

arrange the release as a propaganda move to counteract the Jewish action.

The German Gestapo, meanwhile, relentlessly continued a purge of Denmark's Jews, extending a house-to-house search all along the Danish coast from Copenhagen north to Helsingor.

Reports from Malmo, on the south coast of Sweden opposite Denmark, said that the Nazis were trying to run down Jews hiding along the coast for an opportunity to escape across the narrow sound to Sweden.[43]

Despite the initial success of the rescue effort, and the exhortation of Danish leaders to help the Jews, the Jews were still in peril. Denmark is a small country, bordered only by Germany and the sea. Eichmann was correct when he stated that Jews who remained in Denmark would eventually be caught. Sweden was the only conceivable haven for the Danish Jews, and the only conceivable escape route was by boat across the Øresund. The Danes knew that, and so did the Nazis.

Chapter Five

THE EXODUS

DENMARK CONSISTS of the Jutland Peninsula and islands to the east. Jutland, extending northward from Germany toward Nazi-occupied Norway, provided no means of escape. Zealand, the largest of the islands and the home of Copenhagen, offered the best chance. Sweden—the only unoccupied country within four hundred sea miles—was tantalizingly close to Copenhagen and the rest of Zealand's eastern shore. North of Copenhagen, where small fishing villages dotted the coastline, Sweden is as little as three miles away. The distance from Copenhagen to Sweden is only about twelve miles. But Sweden, which just days earlier had conditioned its acceptance of Denmark's Jews on Nazi Germany's consent, had yet to open its doors to a mass influx of refugees.

The Nazi occupation of Denmark and Norway in 1940 isolated Sweden and left it in a precarious state. Sweden's priority was to keep itself out of the war and keep German troops out of Sweden. From that point of view, its reluctance to do anything that might provoke Nazi retaliation was understandable. Something more persuasive than Duckwitz's plea would have to be brought to bear on the Swedish government.

That persuasion came to some degree from the Swedish people. But the final push came from one of the first Danish refugees to reach Sweden—nuclear physicist Niels Bohr. Bohr was a Nobel

41

Prize winner and founder of Copenhagen's Institute for Theoretical Physics. Hans Hedtoft, who was a friend of Bohr and knew that Bohr's mother was part of a prominent Jewish family, warned him about the Nazi plot the same night that Hedtoft was tipped off by Duckwitz. Swiftly, a plan was put into motion to extricate Bohr from Denmark—a plan deemed critical to save Bohr, to deprive the Nazis of his knowledge, and to secure his assistance for the Allies. After being briefly hidden in a Copenhagen home, Bohr, his wife Margrethe, his brother Harold (am eminent mathematician), and Harold's son Ole were led through back streets to a dock where a small fishing boat, the *Søstjernen*, stood ready. The passengers, some hidden in the tiny cabin and others hidden between crates on deck, waited anxiously as the captain, Christian Hansen, struggled to start the engine. The sound of nearby rifle fire added to the sense of urgency. Finally, the one-cylinder diesel sputtered to life, and the *Søstjernen* pulled away from its dock. It was soon plodding through choppy seas to a rendezvous point in the middle of the Øresund, where Captain Hansen waited for a second vessel to arrive. Soon a "larger boat," crewed by "Danish resistance men"—a boat that was much like *Gerda III*, but whose identity remains shrouded in mystery—came alongside to receive the passengers and take them the rest of the way to Sweden.[44]

A police report, typed in Sweden on October 2, 1943, states that Neils Bohr arrived at Limhamn at 5:00 a.m. on September 30, in a vessel containing his party and ten other refugees who it picked up from small boats off the Danish Coast. The chilly reception that awaited them, and over two hundred other Danes who fled to Sweden at the end of September and the start of October without waiting for that country's permission, was also reflected in the police report. As the report stated, Bohr and his fellow travelers were apprehended by military personnel and "immediately taken to the criminal police station."

Upon his arrival at the police station, Bohr identified himself as a physicist with "important messages for the Swedish government." A skeptical but efficient officer quickly confirmed Bohr's credentials with Georg Kahlson, a Swedish science professor and outspoken foe of the Nazis. Once he was vouched for by Kahlson, the police placed Bohr on a 6:55 train to Stockholm.

When Bohr arrived in Stockholm, a British aircraft was already on the ground waiting to take him to London. But Bohr refused to go any further until Sweden "promised refuge to all Danish Jews who were able to reach its shores."[45] After meetings with Sweden's foreign minister and King Gustav V, Bohr received the assurance he was looking for. At 7:00 pm on October 2, Swedish radio announced that the foreign minister had "extended an offer from the Swedish government to receive all of the Danish Jews."[46] As Bohr demanded, the announcement was repeatedly broadcast across the Øresund for all of Denmark to hear.

Bohr's ability to produce so quick a change by the Swedish government on so important an issue, rested on his world-wide reputation as a nuclear physicist, and on the intense desire of the United States and England to have him join their nuclear programs. An article appearing in the October 9, 1943, *New York Times*, reporting on Bohr's arrival in London, stated:

> Dr. Niels H. D. Bohr, refugee Danish scientist and Nobel Prize winner for atomic research, reached London from Sweden today, bearing what a Dane in Stockholm said were plans for a new invention involving atomic explosions.
>
> The plans were described as of the greatest importance to the Allied war effort.[47]

Two months later, on December 8, 1943, Bohr arrived in Washington to meet with General Leslie Graves, the director of the immense United States nuclear weapons effort known as the Manhattan Project. Over the next twenty months, Bohr made a series of extended visits to Los Alamos, where the Manhattan Project's top physicists made the breakthroughs that were required to design and build a working bomb. Chief physicist Robert Oppenheimer credited Bohr with important contributions to the second and larger of the two bombs that were produced—the bomb that the United States dropped on Nagasaki on August 9, 1945, causing Japan to surrender and bringing World War II to an end.

Sweden's announcement that it would provide a refuge to all Danish Jews who reached its shores made a mass escape possible. But hiding thousands of Jews who were being hunted by the Gestapo until passage on a boat could be arranged, getting them to the rescue boats on roads patrolled by the Nazis, and then getting them across the Øresund, remained a daunting task. It was, however, a task that the Danes undertook with remarkable speed.

The flow began as a trickle, even before Sweden officially opened its ports to Jewish refugees. Records kept by the Swedish navy and police force indicate that approximately 125 refugees were transported to Sweden on September 30, and another 100 on October 1. The numbers then grew by leaps and bounds: approximately 250 arrived in Sweden on October 2; another 300 on October 3; another 400 on October 4; another 550 on October 5; and another 700 per day on October 6 and 7. The next two days, October 8 and 9, coincided with Yom Kippur Eve and Yom Kippur Day. These are the times that Jews traditionally gather in synagogues to seek forgiveness for transgressions committed during the past year and to pray, in the words of the Yom Kippur prayer book, to be "inscribed in the book of life" for the coming year. As if to answer that prayer, Danish mariners on those two days transported 2,500 Jews and other family members—1,100 on October 8 and 1,400 on October 9—from Nazi-occupied territory to safety in Sweden. These were, far and away, the two peak days of the rescue operation.[48]

After Yom Kippur, the number of refugees transported each day dropped precipitously, to 400 people on October 10, and to an average of about 220 people per day for the next six days. Another 1,000 refugees were transported during the rest of October and early November.

THE NUMBER OF SUCCESSFUL CROSSINGS obscures the challenges that the rescuers faced. The magnitude of these challenges, and the harsh consequences of failure, were demonstrated by events that took place up and down the Zealand coast when the surge in crossings caught the Gestapo's attention. The first disaster occurred at Gilleleje, a fishing village on the northern tip of Zealand. Gilleleje's harbor, though bigger than most, was in many ways typical of the fishing villages north of Copenhagen. Being man-made harbors, they are surrounded by large seawalls with narrow openings to keep the waves out. The same walls, sometimes topped with fishing shacks and roadways, made it easy for the Gestapo to prevent rescue boats from leaving and to intercept them when they returned. These harbors, which looked so promising on the map, were often the most dangerous in practice.

On October 3, a Gestapo shore patrol intercepted the motor vessel *Dannebrog* as it attempted to leave its Gilleleje dock with nineteen Jews on board. The departure was cut short when the Gestapo agents fired a volley of bullets into the pilot house, forcing the two crew members to leap off the boat. The refugees took control and attempted to press on, but they ran aground before they could get past the stone walls that encircled the harbor. Unable to continue by boat, and unwilling to simply await capture, the Jews followed the crew members into the water. Gestapo agents, reinforced by German troops, arrested the Jews as they climbed ashore. All nineteen were transported to Horserød Prison, a collection point for captured Jews and other Nazi targets, and were then deported to the Theresienstadt concentration camp.[49]

The next day, October 4, the Gestapo struck the fishing village of Snekkersten, twenty-three miles north of Copenhagen, near the narrowest point of the Øresund. With Sweden so close to Snekkersten, Jews flocked there in the hope of finding a boat willing to take them across. Once again, it was not as easy as it seemed on a map. Eight fishing boats loaded with refugees made the trip to Sweden that day. When they returned, the Gestapo was waiting. Gestapo agents seized the first seven boats that returned and imprisoned twelve captured fishermen at Horserød.[50] The crew of the eighth boat, seeing trouble ahead, changed course and escaped. Valdemar Koppel, a Jewish newspaperman whom the Nazis captured during his attempt to reach a rescue boat, was a prisoner at Horserød when the fishermen were brought in. He described them as "a magnificent bunch" who "received rather brutal and harsh treatment" but "refused to lose heart."[51] Koppel also witnessed the arrival of Jews who were caught during attempts to escape from the harbors at Dragør, Kastrup, Gilleleje, and "many other" places.[52]

The Nazis captured the Jews at Dragør, a small fishing village seven miles south of Copenhagen, just hours after they arrested the fishermen at Snekkersten. German soldiers and Gestapo agents entered Dragør—where *Gerda III* was based during peacetime years and where all of its crew members lived—in time to intercept a line of taxis racing toward the docks with Jewish passengers. As a volley of shots rang out, two of the escaping families surrendered, and two boats that had been waiting for them made a getaway into the storm-tossed waters of the Øresund. Other Jewish families ran into the village's narrow lanes where, in the darkness, doors opened and shelter was given until well-organized escapes, for which Dragør became justly famous, could be arranged. One of the homes where Jews were given refuge was that of Drogden Lighthouse keeper Ejler Haubirk Sr., a man whom the rescue fleet and the resistance could count on for support.[*]

---

[*] Despite the setback on October 4, approximately 700 Jews were brought to safety from Dragør by local fishing boats and the town's pilot boat. To avoid being intercepted at the docks, departures often took place from beaches outside of town. Fishing boats approached the shore at night and signaled to refugees, hidden behind shrubs or otherwise camouflaged, to wade toward them. Leo Goldberger, then the thirteen-year-old son of the cantor at Copenhagen's Great Synagogue, and later a professor at New York University, wrote of the experience. He recalled "wading out some hundred feet from shore" in icy water that "reached up to my chest," to "a courageous and noble" Dragør fisherman who lifted his family on board. Along with Leo, the fisherman rescued Leo's older brother, his parents, and two younger brothers whom his father clutched in his arms as they waded toward the boat. (Goldberger, *The Rescue of the Danish Jews,* 164-67; Werner, *A Conspiracy of Decency,* 68.)

Just hours after the Gestapo intercepted the fleeing Jews at Dragør, a passing boat hit a mine a short distance from the harbor and was blown apart by the resulting explosion. It was, quite literally, a powerful reminder of another hazard that confronted the Jews and their rescuers.

On the following night, October 5, the Gestapo returned in force to Gilleleje and prevented boats from leaving the harbor. Many Jews who had already reached town when the Nazis intercepted the *Dannebrog*, and others who continued to arrive by train, had been brought to the attic of the town's church to protect them until departures could resume. Their sanctuary was short-lived. A local woman, who had fallen in love with a Nazi soldier, betrayed them. Shortly after 3:00 a.m., truckloads of Nazi troops surrounded the church with machine guns. Of the approximately eighty Jews in the attic, all but one were captured. The sole exception, a young man named Bruno, climbed a ladder to the bell tower and remained hidden among the bells until daylight when, as one historian described it, rescuers found him "more dead than alive."[53]

A few days later, on October 7, Bruno and nine other Jews left Gilleleje on an open boat and set out to cross the Øresund. They made it only a short distance before the boat took on water and capsized. Five of the passengers—four adults and a little girl—were plucked from the water by a passing boat. Two other escaping Jews swam to shore. Bruno was among three passengers who drowned.[54]

Most of those captured in the church loft, with the notable exception of nineteen-year-old Gert Lilienfeldt, were taken to Horserød Prison and then transported to Theresienstadt. Lillienfeldt managed to escape from his Nazi captors while they were moving him through Denmark. His ongoing attempts to reach safety would lead him to Henny and *Gerda III*.

Although there were no other mass arrests on the scale of Gilleleje, the Gestapo continued its hunt. Among the ongoing reminders of the perils faced by refugees and rescuers was a deadly encounter at Taarbæk Havn, nine miles north of Copenhagen, on October 9. Claus Christian Heilesen, an eighteen-year-old engineering student born to a Jewish mother and Christian father, had organized an escape on the fishing boat *Matador* for himself, his brother, and other Jewish refugees. Taarbæk Havn is another in the chain of man-made harbors on the Danish coast where stone walls reach out from the town and wrap around a tightly packed circle of local vessels. From the buildings that fronted the harbor, and from the road that runs along it, every boat and each path leading to them was readily visible. On October 9, Heilsen's late-night boarding process was largely complete, and the boat was preparing to depart, when Gestapo agents, whom an informer had alerted to the activity in the harbor, reached the water's edge.

There were conflicting, unresolved accounts of what happened next. An unconvincing version asserted that the Gestapo agents fired mere warning shots, with unintentionally fatal effect. More compelling accounts asserted that a firefight erupted between the Gestapo agents and rescuers who attempted to repel them while Heilesen cast off the *Matador*'s dock lines. About the results, however, there was no doubt: Heilesen was shot to death, and thirteen others were captured.

Aage Bertlesen, leader of a highly successful rescue organization known as the Lyngby Group, shed further light on the shooting. Taarbæk Havn is a part of the Lyngby-Taarbæk municipality, Bettlesen's home turf. Addressing the Heilsen shooting, and a clearly intentional assault on a rescue group nineteen days later, Bettlesen recounted:

> I remember a visit to the police station in Lyngby at the beginning of the transports. It was the day after young Heilesen had been shot in Taarbæk harbor while helping Jews in the boats.... The police showed me the bullets they had found, and some pictures of the young man, close ups of him lying on the bridge [leading to the dock] his head blown to pieces. I was not hardened to sights of this kind, and the police pictures touched me deeply.[55]

Bertlesen further revealed that the deadly events at Taarbæk Havn were nearly repeated on the night of October 28, seventeen miles up the coast at Humlebæk, when Bertlesen's group fell into a Nazi trap. An informer, posing as a saboteur on the run from the Nazis, persuaded members of the Lyngby group to engineer his escape. On the evening the escape was to take place, members of the group led him from a waterfront hotel that they used as an operations center toward a fishing boat that had pulled up to the hotel dock with two refugees already on board. When members of the Lyngby Group and their helpers reached the open ground between the hotel and the dock, the informer flashed a light signal to Gestapo agents who were lying in wait. As Bettlesen described it, "the Gestapo men... started shooting at" the rescuers who were leading the way to the boat. At the sound of the gunshots, the fisherman "quickly let go the hawser" and "managed to get himself and his two passengers safely across to Sweden." Several of the shoreside rescuers were captured, while another managed to run behind the hotel and escape over a hill "with bullets whizzing past his ears."[56]

In all, 190 Jews, along with at least a dozen rescuers, were captured during failed escape attempts during October and early November—this in addition to the 284 Jews that the Nazis captured during the Friday night raids that ran from October 1 into the early morning hours of October 2. Overall, the Nazis captured 474 Jews on Danish soil and deported them to the Thereseinstadt concentration camp.[57]

News of the gunfire, arrests, and confiscation of boats spread rapidly through the close-knit communities along the Zealand coast. The four *Gerda III* crew members were certainly well aware of what transpired in their home town of Dragør. None of that deterred *Gerda III*'s crew from throwing themselves into the rescue effort.

For *Gerda III*'s crew, rescuing Jews from the Nazis was an extension—on a much larger scale—of rescue work they had already been performing for one of Denmark's earliest resistance groups. That work was brought about by the crew's ties to the Drogden

Lighthouse keeper, Ejler Haubirk Sr., and his two sons. They were connected by the lighthouse and by their community. They were all Dragør men. Dragør, where *Gerda III* was based before and after the war years, is a classic Danish fishing village. Tile and thatched roof homes from the 17th and 18th centuries are tightly packed, separated by narrow cobblestone lanes. It is a place where families live generation after generation and know whom they can trust. It has a wonderfully timeless quality that bespeaks a love of Danish and local tradition. It was a place where the Nazi occupation was despised and where resistance took root early.

Haubirk's elder son, Ejler Haubirk Jr., was a renowned resistance fighter whose anti-Nazi activity began at the start of the occupation and ended only when the Gestapo ambushed and killed him outside a Copenhagen Cafe in October 1944. His brother Ingolf worked hand-in-hand with him. The Drogden lighthouse, until the Nazis began to use it as an observation post in 1943, was an important asset for their operation.

The lighthouse was a stopping place for pilot boats from the Swedish coast as well as a daily destination for *Gerda III*. When members of the Haubirks' resistance group had to escape from the Nazis, *Gerda III* took them to the lighthouse—a perfect safe house before the Nazis moved in—where they waited for a Swedish boat to bring them the rest of the way. "Thus," as one Danish researcher concluded, "by the time of the rescue in October 1943, the crew [of *Gerda III*] were already used to resistance activity"—and to rescue work in particular.[58]

Henny and the Crew: The Operation on Land

Gerda III's involvement in the Jewish rescue operation began at the very start of October, placing it among the first rescue boats to go into action.

The crew's rescue work for the Haubirk resistance group gave them an edge—experience that virtually no other boat had. But the Jewish rescue operation was different. They would have to transport refugees not just occasionally, but every day. They would have to go not just to the lighthouse, but all the way to the Swedish Coast. They would have to get far more people on board for each trip. And for all of that, they would need Henny's help.

Gerda III's crew gained confidence in Henny during her three years at the Lighthouse and Buoy Service. In the closing days of September, as word of the Nazis' plan to capture the Jews spread throughout Denmark, a crewman asked Henny to meet them on the boat after work. That afternoon, at what would be the end of her last normal workday for years to come, Henny stepped out of her office at the Royal Dockyards and took the few steps to *Gerda III*—a few steps that transported her across the life-changing boundary from passive observer to active resister. All four crew members— Captain Einer Tønnesen, engineer John Hansen, Otto Andersen, and Gerhardt Steffensen—were there to usher her on board and lead her down a ladder into the small crew quarters where they could speak in private.[59] There they began to discuss a plan for saving Jews—hundreds of people who, with few exceptions, they had never met.

The crew had already concluded that *Gerda III* was ideally suited for transporting large numbers of Jewish refugees to Sweden, and had plotted at least one detour from their lighthouse supply route to the Swedish coast. But they needed Henny's help to accomplish two things before they could even begin: to obtain her father's permission to place the boat and those associated with it at risk; and to reposition *Gerda III* from the Royal Dockyards, where it was now surrounded by German warships and troops, to a new base that was more suitable for sneaking refugees aboard.

She required no persuasion. As Henny later stated in a filmed interview, she "felt furious" that the Nazis would "interfere with our Danish people." The Jews, she continued, "were Danes like we were. We never divided [ourselves] up into Danes or Jews. The Danish Jews, they were just Danes."[60]

Henny satisfied the crew's requests and did a great deal more. In the manner in which Danes communicated with family members about resistance activities—which is to say hardly at all—Henny accomplished much in a few words. Seeking to spare her mother the anxiety of knowing what was about to unfold, Henny said nothing at home that evening. The following morning, she went directly to her father's office. Without explicitly stating the purpose, Henny asked her father "to arrange a berth for *Gerda III* on the Christenshavn Canal across from Wilder's Square…."[61] Beyond that, the things she requested from her father were simple: don't search for the vessel when it deviates from its usual route and schedule, and don't make any changes to the crew. Henny's father, fully understanding her intentions, asked only that she "look well after [herself] and not get too deeply involved," an admonition she plainly ignored.[62]

Two days after Henny's initial conversation with *Gerda III*'s crew, they began to operate from a berth on a segment of the canal adjoining Copenhagen Harbor. The canal runs for slightly over half a mile through the heart of Christianshavn. Short perpendicular sections near the middle—where *Gerda III* was located—and at each end of the canal connect it to the harbor. Christianshavn, and the canal running through it, are a short walk from the heart of Copenhagen. A low-lying drawbridge that pedestrians and bicyclists stream across daily, the Knippelsbro Bridge, links Copenhagen with Christianshavn, two-tenths of a mile from where *Gerda III* was repositioned. (A second more distant bridge, the Langebro Bridge, connects Christianshavn's southern tip to Copenhagen.) The canal-front family home that Henny continued to live in with her family was just minutes away, by foot, from both the Knippelsbro Bridge and from *Gerda III*'s new base. It was an area of which Henny knew every inch, and where she knew people who could be trusted—important attributes for an area where many of the tensest moments of the rescue operation would take place.

Gerda III's new berth was located behind a warehouse that was also crucial to the rescue operation's success. Henny later recounted:

> At the end of Strandgade [Strand Street] we had borrowed a warehouse…. On the Strand side there was a door through

which we could enter quickly. On the other side was a gate opening onto the quay, just in front of the place where *Gerda III* was docked.

My task every evening was to look for Jews [who had been taken or directed to rendezvous points] and to guide them to the warehouse, where we hid them.[63]

Hans Just's warehouse, where Henny based Gerda III
and hid Jews in the attic during the rescue mission.
(Photo courtesy of the Dragør Local Archive.)

Bringing Jews to the warehouse, and then onto *Gerda III*, was a complicated task that was fraught with danger. Recounting that process, Henny wrote in 1980 that "it was arranged [for] each refugee, accompanied by no more than one child, to show up at a certain time and place."[64] She added in a 1994 interview that she was given a list "that [she] had to learn by heart with names and addresses of people [she] had to pick up." Henny met them at the designated rendezvous points and took them on foot to homes close to the warehouse—homes "where we allied ourselves with nice helpful people that we could rely upon." At times, *Gerda III* crew members did the same, escorting other people to the Christianshavn safe houses. The Jews who Henny and the crew led along this escape route sometimes had to wait in these homes for three, four, or even five days before they could take the next step to freedom.

Henny sought to accommodate up to fifteen people—the most that could be hidden in the recesses of *Gerda III*—in the warehouse at any one time. To collect more people in the warehouse would increase the danger that they would be discovered by sentries who patrolled the wharf behind the warehouse, or by informers. In the wee hours of each October morning, Henny slipped out of her family home, tip-toeing through a room in which her mother slept, and made the rounds of the safe houses where the Jews who could be transported the next day were waiting. As she described it:

> It became my job at 1:00 in the morning to pick up the refugees—one person at a time, possibly with one child, and relaxedly stroll with them down Strandgade to the Christianshavn Canal. At the end of Strandgade...there was a door at [the side of the warehouse where] we could sneak in.[65]

What little luggage the refugees could bring was taken earlier in the day by *Gerda III* crewmen "Steff" or Andersen.

Waiting in the warehouse to be brought on board *Gerda III* was another tense time. Henny wrote:

> The refugees spent the night in the attic of the warehouse [where]...they had to wait as quiet as mice. The worst time was when we had many children, not to mention infants. We always carried a jar of sleeping pills and almost every night it was necessary to quiet down some children with a pill to get some calm in the group. Food was also taken care of. There was always something to eat or drink for our

'guests' in the attic, but no one could eat, we all had a bad case of stomach ache, and the night seemed endlessly long both for the refugees and the five of us.[66]

For at least one person who waited for salvation on *Gerda III*— the teenager who escaped from the Nazis after being captured in the Gilleleje church attic—the night in the warehouse attic was particularly harrowing.

GERT LILIENFELDT had effectively been on the run for four years, beginning as a fifteen-year-old at the start of World War II. Born in the small German town of Soest, he had experienced the degradations and terror that befell Jews under the Nazi regime. Forced to abandon their home and business, his family moved to Düsseldorf where they tried to live inconspicuously—indeed invisibly—as anti-Semitism continued to engulf them. On November 9, 1938, when Gert was fourteen years old, the orchestrated night of violence that became known as Krystallnacht ("The Night of Broken Glass") swept through Düsseldorf and other cities in Germany and Austria. Nazi mobs smashed the windows and destroyed the contents of businesses that were still in Jewish hands. Synagogues suffered the same fate. In the hours after midnight, Jewish homes were broken into and inhabitants were forced into the streets to be taunted and often beaten by the mob. In a further glimpse of what was to come, 30,000 Jewish men were taken from their families and sent to what later became death camps. It was a moment when many Jews under Hitler's rule abandoned hope that the insanity would end and desperately began seeking means of escape. Gert's parents, who found no way out for themselves, found a way out for him.

Gert's parents placed him in the hands of an organization, Youth Aliyah, that transported thousands of Jewish children between the ages of fourteen and sixteen from Germany and Austria to places of relative safety—putting them at least temporarily beyond Hitler's reach. Although the organization went into high gear after Krystallnacht, it would take nearly a year before Gert could leave Germany. It was a period, in his words, in which "life had become a day-to-day ordeal filled with constant anxiety—anxiety, anxiety, anxiety."[67]

Denmark took in 320 Youth Aliyah children, almost all of them during the first four months of World War II, and another 377 young Jews beyond the age of sixteen. For them, Denmark was meant to be a temporary refuge. The ultimate destinations were agricultural communities ("kibbutzim") that were sprouting up in the portion of Palestine that would later become Israel.[68] The Nazi invasion of Denmark soon after Gert arrived put an end to that plan for him and most other Aliyah children, trapping them in Nazi occupied territory. Responding to the emergency, Danish farm families took in the Aliyah children and treated them as their own, providing security and agricultural training for the lives the children were preparing to lead. On the government level, Denmark gave Gert and other recent arrivals the same protection that it extended to its own citizens. But he had seen the Nazis on their home turf, where they were unrestrained by Danish law, and the dark memories haunted him. Those memories may also have given him the determination he needed to survive.

That determination was put to the test on the night he was captured in Gilleleje and during the days that followed. As the Gestapo stormed the Gilleleje church, Gert attempted to escape onto the roof and, when that proved impossible, raced up the bell tower—only to be captured by Gestapo agents who pursued him. Gert was held for twenty-four hours at Horserød prison, where the Nazis incarcerated him while they made plans to transport Gert to the Theresienstadt concentration camp. While he was being transported, Gert seized another opportunity to break free. He was being moved in a German army truck when it stopped at Dagmarhus, the Gestapo's headquarters in Copenhagen, to unload other prisoners. Seeing his chance, he jumped from the truck and ran. A taxi driver who observed his escape sped to his rescue and, at Gert's request, whisked him away to Øresund Hospital. It was a refuge that Gert already knew well.

Gert had been a patient at Øresund Hospital, nearing the end of treatment for tuberculosis, when the Nazis first attempted to round up and deport Denmark's Jews. The hospital's chief physician, Dr. Blagvad, organized the ill-fated attempt to secure Gert's passage from Gilleleje. When Gert returned following his capture and escape, Dr. Blagvad brought Gert to his home and hid him there for a week while he made arrangements for Gert to escape on *Gerda III*—an escape route that Dr. Blagvad had come to know as one of the surest.

On the night of October 14, nine days after the Nazis had surrounded him with machine guns and captured him in Gilleleje, Gert sat alongside Henny in the Christianshavn warehouse. Now, as he and Henny waited in the warehouse attic, they knew that what happened to him in Gilleleje could happen to them there.

HENNY, THE JEWS, AND THE CREW OF *GERDA III* passed the early morning hours in the warehouse anticipating the moment when the Jews could race through the gate and across the cobblestone covered wharf to the waiting boat—the boat that embodied their hopes and represented their best chance of escaping the Nazis' grasp. But between the warehouse and the boat, one clear obstacle remained. Henny later recounted:

> Our big headache was two German guards who patrolled the quay outside the warehouse, continuously walking back and forth. They would meet right in front of *Gerda III*, turn around, march 100 meters in opposite directions, turn around and meet up again right in front of *Gerda III*. This was nerve racking because we had to make use of the [brief period] when they had turned around and were walking away from each other with their backs to the boat.

By the time Gert made his escape on *Gerda III*, he had the benefit of a well-practiced operation. In the earliest pre-dawn hour that the crew could appear to be readying *Gerda III* for its regular duty, and just minutes before the boarding was to begin, Henny led Gert and the other refugees from the attic to the ground floor of the warehouse. There she arranged them in rows, hidden in darkness behind the gate that faced the wharf, the waiting boat, and—marching back and forth across their path in endless repetition—the two sentries. On board *Gerda III*, the crew carefully watched the sentries march toward the ends of the wharf. When the sentries were as far as they could go before turning back toward the boat—when the chance for the next person to reach *Gerda III* unseen was as good as it was going to get—a crew member signaled Henny to send the next person across. There was no time for coaxing or gentle persuasion, just a push from Henny to propel another person toward the boat and the arms of crewmen who lifted the refugees over the rail and quickly jammed them into the cargo hold.[69]

Dashing into the open from the sanctuary of the warehouse—knowing that German sentries were patrolling to their right and left with rifles at the ready—was a courageous act. Minutes earlier the refugees, in Gert's words, had been frightened stiff in the attic. Now, when their turn came, each man and woman had to leap into action without hesitation. Unable to see anything except the boat that lay before them, they had to put their faith in Henny to thrust them forward at precisely the right moment. And thrust them forward she did.

So it went, person after person, until all of the adults and older children were in the cargo hold. "And when all of the adults were on board," Henny recalled, "we brought the children" who were too small and, in many cases, too heavily sedated to run across on their own. Gert wound up lying on the bottom of the hold with a small child pressed against his chest—a child he hugged throughout the rough, several hour-long, passage.

In an interview fifty years later on *Gerda III*'s deck, Gert recalled Henny's push, his short dash to the boat, and then almost "being thrown into the hold." As he put it, it all "happened so lightning fast."

The escaping adults and children were indeed "jammed" into the hold, as Henny put it. *Gerda III* was built along the lines of a fishing boat, and the cargo hold was designed more with fish in mind than people. The hold, lined with damp wooden inner planks, is ten feet long with an average width of about twelve feet. Barrels and other cargo took up much of the central area. And with a maximum height of four feet at the centerline, and a round bottom that reduced the headroom as you moved outward, there was barely room to sit along the sides of the hull—the only place where a person might go undetected if a sentry looked into the hold. The Jews settled into the tight recesses at the edges of the cargo hold, a row on each side of the boat. They sat with their backs pressed against the inner hull planks to keep themselves as well hidden as possible, and to brace themselves against the roll of the boat as it pounded through choppy seas and sometimes steep waves. When up to fifteen people were "packed tightly into the hold," together with that day's lighthouse supplies, hatch covers were placed over the hold and covered with gear to discourage searches.

Gerda III *Cargo Hold.*

On at least one occasion, Henny and the crew also hid refugees in the small crew cabin at the bow of the boat. *Gerda III* was not built for extended voyages, and the cabin reflected that. The seven-foot-long triangular space, at the base of a short ladder, had just enough room for the crew to huddle around a small stove on a winter day, or to rest in narrow upper and lower berths attached to each side of the hull.

Hiding refugees in the crew quarters may have been compelled on occasion by an even greater than usual sense of urgency or by a shortage of space in the cargo hold. Whatever the cause, placing refugees in the crew cabin was a bold move. The entrance was covered by a sliding hatch that could easily be pushed open for a look below. Four six-inch diameter portholes, one on each side of the slightly elevated cabin top, provided other opportunities to peer below—at least for someone diligent enough to get on his hands and knees and aim a light through the glass. Using the crew cabin appears to have been a departure from the carefully thought-out escape plan—and probably a rare one—but a vivid account by another teenage refugee, Aaron Engelhardt, makes clear that it was done.

When the refugees had all been led to their onboard hiding places, and the crew had done everything possible to conceal their presence, *Gerda III* was ready to depart. But the boat and the Jews hidden below deck still had to wait. Henny explained:

> The boat couldn't cast off until seven o'clock in the morning. When it started its engine the two Germans on duty came on board to check the papers. They never thought to go down to the hold where they would have found our Jewish guests. Every morning the crew offered a beer to the two soldiers; they toasted each other and talked about the weather. Then the Germans went back on the quay.[70]

The German sentries sat on the hatch covers above the cargo hold to drink their beers. The escaping Jews listened to the sentries' toasts and chatter about the weather—all the while hiding with their heads inches beneath the sentries' boots.[71]

Henny watched this daily departure ritual from a hiding place inside the warehouse, staying just long enough to see *Gerda III* leave the canal entrance and, with the approaching autumn sunrise beginning to illuminate its path, turn toward the open waters that separated Denmark from Sweden. Within four months, Henny would be forced to flee across the Øresund to save her own life. But for now, as *Gerda III* headed to sea, Henny headed home to rest and prepare for the next night's mission. It was a process, Henny wrote, that went on "every night, many weeks in a row."[72]

AARON ENGELHARDT provided a description of these events, and more, from a refugee's perspective. His narrative, preserved by the Copenhagen City Archive, starts with a knock on the door of the apartment that Aaron lived in with his parents and his four younger brothers and sisters—and with the start of their life in exile.

Aaron was a few weeks short of his fifteenth birthday when the manager of his apartment complex came to warn his family that the Nazis were about to pounce and that they had to leave at once to save themselves. The manager, who he identified only as Miss Bendtsen, went a step further. Her apartment in a neighboring building became the Engelhardts' first hiding place—the place where they spent their first night as a hunted family.

The next day the family split up and found shelter in four different homes—a temporary measure while plans for a mass evacuation to Sweden were still being formulated. Days later, Aaron's father gathered his family in a taxi and brought them to Copenhagen's Bispebjerg Hospital.

Following instructions that were transmitted to him through a growing network of Danish rescue groups, Aaron's father brought the family to the chapel at the center of the hospital's sprawling complex. From there they were led through underground passages to a large basement conference room that, in Aaron's words, "already contained many Jews"—all waiting in silence for information about the next step in their escape. Any lingering hopes of leaving Denmark that day were dashed a few hours after nightfall when a doctor informed them that "there were too many Germans on the road" to go anywhere and that they would have to "stay overnight and then see what could be done" the next day. Aaron and his family were later brought to the hospital's nursing quarters to sleep and steel themselves for whatever came next.

Aaron's account, coupled with other sources, suggests that his family arrived at Bispebjerg Hospital on October 7, after hiding in people's homes for at least a week. The prior day Dr. Karl Køster, the principal organizer of the hospital's rescue effort, spread the word that Jews in search of an escape route should find their way to the chapel at 9:00 a.m. under the guise of attending a funeral. Arrangements had been made to transport forty Jews, the number expected to arrive that morning, from the chapel to rescue boats. The estimate was way off. At least 140 Jews streamed into the chapel the first day the plan was put into operation, many by 9:00 a.m. and others later in the day. The sudden influx required the hospital to improvise a plan to hide and feed the additional hundred people until boats could be secured for them. By 10:00 p.m., many of the refugees had been assigned to patient beds—complete with fictitious patient names and medical charts—in wards above the conference room. Then, just as Aaron described it, the remaining families and other refugees were hidden in thirty apartments within the nurses' quarters. The next day, another two hundred Jewish refugees arrived and were hidden in wards and in 130 apartments in the nurses' quarters.[73]

When the roads were once again passable, and an escape had been arranged for the Engelhardts on *Gerda III*, an ambulance brought Aaron and the rest of his family to rendezvous points around Copenhagen—seemingly random points that would not draw the attention that would be aroused if ambulances had arrived day after day at *Gerda III*'s dock, at the warehouse, or at the safe houses that Henny had arranged in Christianshavn.

Describing his final steps from the warehouse to *Gerda III*, Aaron wrote:

> One by one we were brought on the boat. Toddlers have gotten their sleeping pills so that they would not cry. Mom, Nina, Sima and I came into the small crew cabin

along with a few others. [Inside the cabin] there was a very nervous man smoking cigarettes....

My father, Rudi and Miriam were put into the cargo hold. Suddenly I heard a child crying and a baby was handed down to me directly under the hatch. I cradled the child and it calmed down.

The next thing Aaron recalled was the "tramp of boots on the deck and the sound of German voices"—the daily sentry visit that the refugees were undoubtedly warned about but that was frightening nonetheless. And then "finally we set sail out into the harbor."

On the escape route that *Gerda III* travelled that day (a route that can be pieced together from Aaron's writing), it would have taken at least an hour for *Gerda III* to begin distancing itself from the Danish shore, and hours more before Aaron and his family reached the safety of Sweden.

Aaron Engelhardt, second from the right in the last row, in a 1945 class photograph taken at the Danish School in Gothenberg Sweden. Leo Goldberger, whose escape from Dragør is described earlier, is in the same row at the left. (Photograph Courtesy of Leo Goldberger.)

On October 18, employees of the Danish Social Services agency entered the apartment that the Engelhardt family had to flee so rapidly. In a practice that was repeated in empty apartments and homes throughout Copenhagen, the Engelhardts' belongings were carefully inventoried, and arrangements were made to preserve everything until the day—one the Danes were sure would come—when their Jewish countrymen could return to their homes. The inventory of the Engelhardt apartment is more than a property list; it is a window into the lives that the Nazis sought to end. For a bedroom that the five Engelhardt children apparently shared, the inventory included two bunk beds and one cot. It also included one microscope, one telescope, and a virtual laboratory equipped with "lots of chemicals and chemical equipment." Crowded in an apartment in the Valby section of Copenhagen, Aaron and his siblings had all the room, intellectual curiosity, and support that they needed to become budding scientists. And then, with the knock on their door, their goal became simple survival.

Finding Henny: The Underground Network

Henny and the crew had the right vessel in the right place for the rescue mission, and they knew how to use it. What they knew less about was how to contact Jews who were already in hiding, and how to avoid contact with informers. How did they establish the "certain time and place" at which to meet people they had never known? Where did Henny get the "list…with names and addresses" that she had to learn by heart before leaving on her daily rounds? Through what channels did three hundred Jews find their way to Henny?

The information and contacts that Henny needed were supplied, in large part, by a resistance group led by Jørgen Kieler. Kieler was a medical student at the University of Copenhagen when the Nazis invaded Denmark. By January 1943, Kieler put his medical training on hold and threw himself into the growing resistance movement. It was a time, Kieler later wrote, when Danes realized that an occupied people must choose between "collaboration with the enemy and active resistance," and they overwhelmingly chose the latter.[74] Kieler turned his Copenhagen apartment into an underground press office and a meeting place for like-minded students. By October 1943, he had developed a core group of fifteen people, mostly medical and law students, that included his brother and two sisters.

On the evening of October 1, Kieler met with his group to plan a response to the Nazis' attack on the Jews. Some members of the group joined other organizations that were establishing escape routes. Jørgen and six other members decided to establish a route of their own.

Jørgen's contacts in the underground press and medical community provided links to Jews who were in hiding places or on the run throughout the country.

Anticipating that some mariners would have to be paid to turn from fishing and other occupations to rescue work, Kieler also raised a large sum of cash for transportation costs as well as bribes and other anticipated expenses. On the morning of October 2, two members of Kieler's group—a twenty-year-old engineering student named Klaus Rønholt and Jørgen's twenty-five-year-old sister Elsebet— began making rounds of estates on the outskirts of Copenhagen to solicit donations. Jørgen reported that Klaus and Elsebet returned on Sunday with "one million Kroner, a considerable fortune." Putting that into context, Elsebet told an interviewer that "after the tour I had two envelopes hidden in my bureau at home. One held the million for the transportation of the Jews, the other held a month's allowance from my parents—twenty kroner." Modestly discounting her own considerable role, Elsebet stated that Klaus, "knew all the families we visited" and "must be given the credit for this trip; it was all his work."[75]

Jørgen Kieler, a meticulous planner, also prepared for hazardous encounters that bribes could not resolve. As part of the decree imposing martial law, the Nazis had ordered Danes to surrender privately held weapons to the police. Jørgen concluded that it was now time to withdraw some of those weapons from the police stockpiles. On October 1, he travelled to his family's home ground on Jutland to meet with the local constable. In Jørgen's words, he and a companion from his group were "very well received by Chief Constable Simony, who gave us seven pistols and ammunition, commenting: 'At your disposal gentlemen. No one is saying that they should only be used to protect transports of Jews.'" In an obvious reference to the growing resistance activity, the Chief Constable added that "they can also be used for other things."[76] In time, they were.

Well connected, well-funded, and well-armed, all that Jørgen and his group lacked was a boat.

That need was partially satisfied by Ebba Lund, a twenty-two-year-old member of Jørgen Kieler's group who proved adept at recruiting fishermen to transport the refugees. In the early days of October, she assembled a small fleet of fishing boats—as many as twelve at any one time—to ferry Jews to Sweden. At the beginning of the emergency, however, she did not know a single boat owner, and the fishermen she recruited—fishermen whose ability to support their families rested on their daily catch—often expected to be paid passage fees that could have depleted Kieler's funds before the job was done. Henny had a boat on day one and did not charge the Jews for its services.

As employees of the Danish Lighthouse and Buoy Service, *Gerda III*'s crew members were able to throw themselves into the rescue effort without worrying about the loss of fishing revenues or the cost and availability of precious war-time fuel. And neither the crew nor anyone else involved in *Gerda III*'s rescue work had any interest in profiting from the Jews' plight—something that would have been anathema to them.

Jørgen and Henny were perfectly positioned to meet each other's needs by joining forces, and they did so. Kieler wrote in a 1987 publication:

> Through their personal contacts, two young girls, Ebba Lund and Henny Sinding, who had joined our group, got in touch with several fishermen and the crew of a

small supply ship [*Gerda III*] which made daily tours to a lighthouse in the middle of the sound between Denmark and Sweden. In this way we established two important escape routes from Copenhagen. Finding Jews, bringing them to the harbor, and organizing and protecting their embarkation became our most important tasks during the following weeks. Ebba and Henny were always there to see them on board. We found ourselves in an emergency situation where risks had to be taken....

About 1,500 persons were rescued via our two routes, without the loss of a single life.[77]

As these numbers suggest, Henny could not have found a better group with which to join forces.

Composed largely of medical students (including Jørgen Kieler, his brother Flemming, and Cato Bakman), they had close associates at hospitals—particularly Bispebjerg Hospital—that sheltered the Engelhardts and nearly two thousand other Jews during the rescue effort.[78]

In the days following the disclosure of the Nazis' plan to capture Denmark's Jews, hospitals sprang to the forefront of the effort to save them. No hospital did more than Bispebjerg. Under the leadership of Dr. Køster, virtually the entire staff participated in the plan to conceal Jews in the hospital's wards and nurses' quarters while the hospital secured passage for them on rescue boats.[79]

Bispebjerg Hospital, located nearly five miles from Christianshavn, also had a ready-made solution to the problem of transporting Jews to rescue boats and rendezvous points. It was perilous to move refugees through miles of Nazi-patrolled Copenhagen streets in daylight, and at least equally dangerous at night when a Nazi-imposed curfew, effective at 8:30 p.m., rendered almost any movement illegal and made easy prey of violators. Ambulances, such as the one that transported Aaron Englehart and his family from Bispebjerg Hospital to Henny, were a nearly perfect solution. Bispebjerg assigned at least one of its own ambulance drivers to transporting refugees full time, and also enlisted the services of a nearby ambulance and firefighting brigade managed by Christian Kisling. Kisling was destined to play significant roles in the rescue and the armed resistance movement. With respect to the rescue, he was an eager and much sought-after participant. As he put it in a 1971 recording, the doctors "trusted me," and "didn't take long to talk to me" about helping Jews escape."[80]

Kisling transported up to fourteen Jews and other Nazi targets at a time in the back of his ambulance. On some occasions, the initial destination was his own garage, where he hid passengers in an attic above the ambulances and fire engines before driving them early the next morning to boats that he had secured for their passage. On other occasions, the destinations were rendezvous points where fellow rescuers such as Henny waited to escort the refugees on the final leg of their escape. Speaking of this aspect of his work in his 1971 recording, in terms that mesh with Henny's description of her routine, Kisling stated that he "was supposed to bring them to a certain spot and they were going to be picked up by somebody else and taken to the boat."

Conveying the tension and uncertainty that attended this leg of the escape route, Kisling described being confronted as he neared the rendezvous point on his first such mission by "a German guard—a very mean fellow…with a machine gun—who demanded to know who was in the vehicle." Kisling responded by shouting "is everything all right," while pointing the ambulance's spotlight in the guard's face. While the guard was momentarily blinded by the light, Kisling "backed the ambulance away…with the light still in [the guard's] face" and sped off. After "cruising around for a while," he completed the rendezvous.

The recording that Kisling left for posterity doesn't name the persons who awaited his passengers at the rendezvous points, or the boats to which his passengers were taken. But for some who passed through Bispebjerg Hospital to *Gerda III* and freedom, Kisling's ambulance was likely to have been a vital link in the chain. Kisling and Henny's group worked in close proximity, in inter-dependent activities, with many of the same contacts at Bispebjerg Hospital and elsewhere. In light of all that, coming together—in the Jewish rescue operation, in their subsequent rescue of Allied airmen and Danish resisters, and in their coming roles as fellow saboteurs—would have been hard to avoid. That their paths crossed is certain. Henny explicitly acknowledged, in commenting on a heroic action that Kisling performed for Henny's resistance group a few months after the Jewish rescue operation, that Kisling had "often" been of help.

Keiler's associate Cato Bakman worked hand-in-hand with Dr. Køster, the leader of Bispebjerg Hospital's rescue operation, to save Jews and other Nazi targets throughout October 1943 and beyond. Given Bakman's close relationship with Kieler—they had worked together in the underground press since January 1943—the escape routes that Kieler provided through Henny and Ebba Lund had to be at the top of Bakman's list. And for Kieler and Henny, the hospital's ability to draw the refugees together and transport them by ambulance to any designated meeting place, at any time of day or night, made the hospital an ideal conduit.

As publishers of an underground newspaper, Kieler's group also had close ties to Mogens Staffeldt, a leader of the underground press. As soon as Duckwitz disclosed the need for the rescue, Staffeldt transformed his Copenhagen bookstore into an organizing center for the rescue effort—a place that Jews and those providing them with sanctuary could turn to for help. Staffeldt's bookstore quickly became another major hub for rescue activity. During October and November 1943, an estimated six hundred Jews passed through the back room of the store, from which they were directed to *Gerda III* and other vessels.[81] As was true of Dr. Køster's hospital team, and of *Gerda III*'s crew, evacuating Denmark's Jews was only one facet— albeit a very large facet—of Staffeldt's efforts to save people from the Nazis. He later stated:

> I was helping people in trouble. I did the same for Jews as I did for Allied fliers, saboteurs and others who had to get to Sweden.[82]

It was, he said, "my duty as a Dane and as a human being."[83]

Echoing Henny's words, Staffeldt stated that Jews who came to his store were told to rendezvous "at a certain time and place" with associates who would lead them to rescue vessels—this at a time when Staffeldt, Kieler, and Kieler's fledgling resistance group were forging a tight bond.[84] They were on a common trajectory, from underground publishers, to rescuers, to leaders of the armed resistance—and they would travel that path together.

By contrast to Jørgen Kieler's relationship with Staffeldt and the medical students in Kieler's resistance group, Jørgen and Henny lived in different worlds prior to October 1943—Jørgen's centered on the elite university where he studied medicine and Henny's centered on the Lighthouse and Buoy Service where she went to work after high school. Their worlds were joined by a common purpose—the rescue of the Jews—and by Mix, the naval cadet who had been held captive at the Drogden Lighthouse and who, by the time the rescue operation got underway, was already helping Kieler turn his student group into a potent armed resistance force. During the month-long rescue and the three subsequent months, Jørgen, Mix, and Henny remained bound in ever more dangerous pursuits that would leave one of them dead, another gravely injured, and the third in exile.

The Crew: Crossing the Øresund

In *Gerda III*'s pilot house, Captain Tønnesen had much to think about, and critical choices to make, as he left the Christianshavn dock with the Jewish refugees hidden below deck. The one certainty was the need to complete the forbidden crossing to Sweden before *Gerda III* arrived at the Drogden Lighthouse. With German lookouts stationed at the Lighthouse, it would have been foolhardy to open the hatches and unload supplies with the refugees still in the cargo hold. And so, as Henny put it, "on the way" to the lighthouse the crew "went over to the Swedish coast [and] got the refugees safely onto the shore." *Gerda III* then had to resume its trip to the lighthouse with all the speed it could muster—seeking to arrive at a time and from a direction that could be squared with its official duties.[85]

Everything else—*Gerda III*'s destination in Sweden, its route, even whether it turned north or south when leaving the Christianshavn dock—involved a more complicated calculus. With changes in the weather and German naval activity, among other things, the best choice one day might be far less desirable the next.

Rescue boats operating from Copenhagen and the cluster of harbors surrounding it transported refugees to five principal destinations, ranging from Barsebäckshamn to Skanör, on the Swedish coast.

The Øresund and (in lower right) the Baltic Sea.
(Drawn by Marjorie Rosenthal.)

The fishing village of Barsebäckshamn was the northernmost alternative and was closest to *Gerda III*'s starting point. Progressing southward, the other possibilities were the large port at Malmö, the small fishing harbors at Limhamn and Klagshamn, and, at the very southwest tip of Sweden, Skanör. Neither Henny nor the crew ever recorded the routes or destinations that they used during the rescue operation. Fortunately, the two young refugees who wrote about their escapes on *Gerda III*, Gert Lilienfeldt and Aaron Engelhardt, did so. Their accounts establish that *Gerda III* brought refugees to the Swedish ports at both the northern and southern ends of the spectrum: Barsebäckshamn and Skanör.

The choice of destinations dictated *Gerda III*'s course from the moment it left its Christianshavn wharf. Although Christianshavn is part of Copenhagen's metropolitan area, it is on an island, Amager, that is separated from central Copenhagen by a nine-mile-long waterway. That waterway, which is narrow and canal-like for much of its length, widens into Copenhagen Harbor on its northern end, where *Gerda III* was docked during the rescue operation, and into a shallow expanse on its southern end. The main entrance to Copenhagen harbor, and the only way in or out for any vessel much larger than *Gerda III*, was to the north. Heading northward through the main harbor and then out into the Øresund offered every advantage—except perhaps stealth—for vessels heading to Sweden.

During World War II, vessels the size of *Gerda III* could also reach the sea by running in the other direction as they left the harbor, passing under the draw bridges that link Christinshavn to the heart of Copenhagen, and then motoring southward through the long, narrow channel to reach the sea at Amager's southern shore. Thanks to Gert Lilienfeldt and Aaron Engelhardt, we know that *Gerda III* did both.

Skanör

Aaron wrote that after "sailing out into the harbor" *Gerda III* immediately turned "south, passing under the Knippelsbro Bridge and then under the Langebro Bridge"—the two draw bridges that spanned the harbor between Copenhagen and Christianshavn. Through a slit under the hatch cover, he added, he could "see German soldiers patrolling the bridges" as *Gerda III* passed beneath them.

Gerda III had to continue south for four and one-half miles, through a waterway that was never more than a few hundred feet wide, before reaching a buoyed channel that ran through the shallow waters of the mile-wide lower estuary. It would be another three and one-half miles before *Gerda III* reached the open sea.

Aaron wrote "how many hours we sailed I do not know." But he vividly recalled "coming on deck to see the Promised Land coming closer and closer"—finally reaching shore "at the small Swedish town of Skanör."

The number of hours that Aaron and other refugees travelled en route to Skanör, and the rough conditions that some of them experienced, can be reconstructed from nautical charts and meteorological almanacs for the period. The first eight miles of the journey, when *Gerda III* motored between the Nazi patrolled shores of the confined waterway, would have lasted about one hour. After leaving the buoyed channel and entering open waters— where *Gerda III* was first exposed to the full force of the wind and waves—Captain Tønnesen would have begun a slow turn to the southeast, keeping the Amager coast and the band of shoals surrounding it to port. At the time of his turn, Skanör lay just over seventeen and one-half miles ahead—at least two hours away in the best of circumstances and considerably more in the rough seas that persisted through much of October. About five and one-half miles after the turn toward Sweden, *Gerda III* would finally leave the Danish coast astern, putting miles between its Jewish passengers and the Gestapo forces on shore. In another seven and one-quarter miles, *Gerda III* would enter Swedish waters. For the crew, those seven and one-quarter miles, in which German naval vessels could have appeared at any time, might well have been the greatest concern.

As long as *Gerda III* travelled through the shipping channels that the Lighthouse and Buoy Service maintained, and was on a path to or from the Drogden Lighthouse, Captain Tønnesen could argue his way past any Nazi vessel that challenged it. At times he did just that. Henny wrote that *Gerda III* was followed and hailed by German patrol boats "once in a while" as it made its way through Danish waters before making a tell-tale turn toward Sweden. Each time, Captain Tønnesen managed to avoid close inspection by shouting that *Gerda III* was "the lighthouse cutter, doing what it had been ordered to do"—supplying the lighthouse and maintaining the navigation aids that marked the channels and shoals along Denmark's shores.[86] That argument evaporated once *Gerda III* motored away from the lighthouse and Danish waters toward Skanör. The direct route from the southern tip of Amager to Skanör passed well south of the Drogden Lighthouse, never coming within three miles of it. If a German vessel intercepted *Gerda III* during the final seven and one-quarter mile slog to Sweden's territorial waters, or the additional four and three-quarter miles to Sweden's coast if German vessels ignored the demarcation line, the crew would be without excuses.

For the Jews hidden below deck, high winds and waves often prolonged the tension and made for a rough ride. During the early days of the rescue, the winds were especially severe, and they were blowing northward from the Baltic directly into the Øresund.

Denmark maintained weather stations at lightships and lighthouses around its coast, including the Drogden Lighthouse. Denmark's Nautical Meteorological Annual for 1943 contains wind and wave data that, its pages note, were recorded daily by lighthouse keeper "E. Haubirk." Haubirk's entries for October 4, 5, and 6—some of the busiest days of the rescue effort—reveal a fearsome start to the month. Winds on October 4 were blowing from the south southwest at Force 7 on the Beaufort scale. At Force 7, winds blow at 28 to 33 knots (32 to 38 miles per hour). The Beaufort scale correlates wind speeds with sea states. At Force 7, according to the scale, "sea[s] heap up" and "white foam from breaking waves begins to blow in streaks." Studies show that wave heights in the area that *Gerda III* traversed during its October 1943 rescue missions average between 2 and 2.5 meters in Force 7 winds, less than the 4 to 6 meters that would be generated on the open ocean but still considerable for a boat whose deck slopes from its high bow to a height of only one meter above the waterline in the area of the cargo hold. Over the next two days, October 5 and 6, winds abated only slightly, to Force 6, and continued to blow from the south-southwest or southwest. At Force 6, winds blow at 22 to 27 knots (25 to 31 miles per hour), generating "whitecaps everywhere [and] more spray."[87]

Once *Gerda III* left the sheltered waterway and turned toward Sweden, it had no shelter from the wind or waves until it reached port. During the seventeen and one-half mile open water passage to Skanör, the boat would have taken the waves nearly broadside, causing it to roll sharply as wave after wave passed under it, breaking waves washed over its deck, and spray pelted the windows of the pilot house.

On eight subsequent days during October, including four straight days from October 11 to 14, *Gerda III* encountered southeast winds of Force 4 or above, conditions that typically generate waves of 1.25 meters and "numerous whitecaps."[88] Although the conditions were far better than the early days of the month, the Jews hidden in the darkness of the cargo hold would still have had to brace themselves against the inner planks of the hull as *Gerda III* rolled in the waves—all the while praying that the trip would not be interrupted by a German patrol boat or a mine.

Gerda III in her World War II configuration plowing through the Øresund in conditions typical of the rescue period. (Photograph Courtesy of the Dragør Local Archive.)

Barsebäckshamn

Gert Lilienfeldt travelled a far different route, with its own set of perils. His account establishes that *Gerda III* took him from Christianshavn to Barsebäckshamn. He crossed in mid-month, after the near-gales of early October had subsided, and he was in more sheltered waters than the refugees experienced on the way to Skanör. Yet he recalled an "endlessly" long passage in which *Gerda III* rolled in the waves while he, all the while, held on to the small seasick child that had been handed down to him.[89]

The trip to Barsebäckshamn began with a somber reminder of the powerful forces arrayed against those onboard. Upon leaving the dock, Captain Tønnesen would have turned north toward the main harbor entrance. That course took *Gerda III* past the Royal Dockyards—where German warships berthed near the wreckage of the Danish navy—before *Gerda III* left the harbor and motored into the Øresund.

From *Gerda III*'s berth on the Christianshavn Canal, a direct route to Barsebäckshamn was about fourteen miles—a little less than two miles north to the harbor entrance and then about twelve miles across the Øresund. It was a distance that *Gerda III* could cover in good conditions in less than two hours.[90] For a Copenhagen fishing boat that had no prescribed route and no scheduled stops during its workday, Barsebäckshamn was a logical destination. It was, in fact, used by the fishing boats that Ebba Lund recruited to transport refugees for the same resistance group that directed refugees to Henny.[91] But for *Gerda III*, which had to take supplies south to the Drogden Lighthouse—where German lookouts as well as Danish lighthouse workers awaited their arrival—it was a different story.

A direct course to Barsebäckshamn required *Gerda III* to depart sharply from its authorized route—heading east northeast instead of southward—as soon as it left Copenhagen's Harbor. That departure would have taken place in one of the most closely watched areas on the Zealand coast. Naval vessels and shore stations combined with Middelgrund Fort, an island fortress two miles from the main harbor entrance, to guard the approaches to Copenhagen. Worse yet, Middelgrund Fort is right on the route from Copenhagen to Barsebäckshamn. *Gerda III* made regular stops at Middelgrund to service two small lighthouses on the island and was therefore known to the German troops stationed there. It was risky to motor past those same troops in a direction in which *Gerda III* had no legal tasks to perform, a direction in which the next lighthouse and buoys—marking the approach to Barsebäckshamn—were miles into Swedish waters. It was risky but, as we know from Gert Lilienfeldt, it was done.

In his interview on the fiftieth anniversary of the rescue, Gert spoke of the tension that gripped everyone in the cargo hold until they reached the destination. For Gert the tension was not fully relieved even when a crew member opened the cargo hatch and proclaimed "we are in Sweden." In his words:

It was not until I set foot on the quay and saw some uniformed Swedish Police that I dared to accept it as true and I felt a sense of relief—an incredibly strong sense of relief.

Only seconds went by before he collected himself sufficiently to thank *Gerda III's* crew for what they had done, but by then it was too late. "As I turned around to look back at the boat it was already heading out of the harbor."

The routes to the more southerly ports were longer but in some significant ways safer. Thanks to Aaron Engelhardt, we know that Captain Tønnesen and his crew chose at least one of them. It is likely that they used at least one more.

Limhamn and Klagshamn

Because the accounts written by Gert Lilienfeldt and Aaron Engelhardt relate to only two of *Gerda III's* many crossings during the month-long rescue operation, it is possible that Captain Tønnesen and his crew headed for other ports on other days. Having established that they travelled to the most northerly and southerly ports used by Copenhagen rescue boats, there is good reason to believe that they also used intermediate destinations—Limhamn, where Neils Bohr was put ashore, and Klagshamn—that could have offered significant advantages on some days.

The distance from Christianshavn to either Limhamn or Klagsman is approximately twenty miles, about five miles shorter that the Skanör route, enabling *Gerda III* to arrive at the lighthouse closer to schedule. Limhamn and Klagshamn had other advantages that went beyond mileage comparisons.

They were the two main destinations for the fourteen or fifteen Dragør boats, manned by neighbors of *Gerda III's* crewmen, that took part in the rescue operation. Frequent passages by Dragør captains and crews would have provided a useful stream of fresh intelligence to Captain Tønnesen and his crew. At least one *Gerda III* crewman, Gerhardt Steffensen, could turn to somebody even closer than a neighbor—he could turn to his brothers. Hans Steffensen was the captain of a pilot boat based in Dragør. Paralleling Gerhardt's activity on *Gerda III*, Hans turned his pilot boat into another significant rescue craft, carrying up to thirteen Jews at a time from Dragør to Sweden. Gerhardt's younger brother Martin, a Dragør fisherman, transported Jews on his fishing boat. Gerhardt's uncle and cousins, all Dragør fishermen, did the same. Were that not enough, lighthouse keeper Haubirk used his vantage point, eighteen meters above the sea, to collect information for rescue and resistance craft about German naval activity in the waters between Dragør and Sweden.[92]

Dragør's rescue boats favored Klagshamn early in the rescue, and then shifted to Limhamn. *Gerda III*'s crew may well have done the same, although Limhamn had some advantages from the start. It was also a port with which the Steffensen brothers seemed particularly comfortable. Later in the war, well after the Jewish rescue was completed, Gerhardt Steffensen teamed up with his brother Martin to smuggle weapons from the Swedish coast to the Danish resistance—and they did so from Limhamn.[93]

Whether bound for Limhamn or Klagshamn, *Gerda III* would have followed the same route for the first ten miles—the route it almost certainly followed at the start of its routine lighthouse supply missions. That route, much like the route to Barsebäckshamn, would have begun with a northerly run through Copenhagen Harbor and out into the Øresund.

South of Copenhagen, the Øresund is divided by Saltholm Island, 4.4 miles of low lying and mostly uninhabited land surrounded by shoals. The island and shoals create a seven-mile-long barrier that closely parallels the Amager coast. Drogden Channel, one of the Øresund's major shipping channels, runs through the gap. Although *Gerda III* could theoretically have passed on either side of Saltholm Island, sticking to Drogden Channel appears to have been the safer choice. Motoring southward through the paired buoys that mark the channel, *Gerda III* would have been right at home. Maintaining the channel markers was part of its routine, and Drogden Channel, not surprisingly, leads directly to the Drogden Lighthouse.

For the refugees hidden below deck, the Drogden Channel would have remained uncomfortably close to Denmark's shores—often no more than half a mile off *Gerda III*'s starboard side—for the ten and one-half mile run from the Copenhagen harbor entrance to Dragør. But throughout that part of the passage, *Gerda III* would have been exactly where it was supposed to be—well positioned to respond to any challenges from German patrol boats.

Past Dragør, the Amager coastline turns sharply west. For another mile, *Gerda III* would have continued down the Drogden channel, with shoals to the right and left of it. Then, with Amager growing more distant, and the Drogden Lighthouse still two and one-half miles ahead, *Gerda III* would reach the southern end of the shoals and could turn east toward Sweden. To the refugees in the cargo hold, the long-awaited turn would have been unmistakable—a dramatic change in the boat's motion being the telltale sign in the dark, windowless cargo hold.

A boat heading down the Drogden Channel during the near gale conditions of early October and the brisk mid-October winds would have had some shelter from the wind and waves until it passed Dragør. For the next mile, until the earliest possible turning point, it would have taken the full force of the wind on its starboard bow, and would have pitched and rolled in the waves that washed over the Amager shoals. After it made the turn toward Sweden, it would have been fully exposed to the wind and waves—but only for half the length of the long open water passage to Skanör. En route to Limhamn, the boat would have taken the waves on its starboard quarter, lifting the stern and causing the boat to roll as each wave passed under it. A boat headed to Klagshamn would have taken the waves nearly broadside, causing a more violent roll.

For the miles that remained beyond the eastward turn to Sweden, a little under eight miles to Klagshamn or about eight and one-half miles to Limhamn, *Gerda III* would again be in open waters and the crew—if they were intercepted by a German vessel—would again be without excuses.

Success at Sea

The proximity of Nazi forces on the Danish coast, the German Navy's control of the sea, the danger of striking a mine, and the sometimes severe pitching and rolling of the boat, meant that fear continued to grip the refugees long after they pulled away from the Christianshavn wharf.

But the reality—which few could have realized at the time—was that a strong boat such as *Gerda III*, built to take the pounding waves that come to the Øresund in autumn, was a place of relative safety. The dangers of being intercepted on Danish soil, where the Gestapo zealously pursued Jews and their rescuers, far exceeded the dangers of being captured or killed at sea. Acknowledging these facts, of course, does nothing to detract from the courage of the Danish rescuers on shore. Nor does it detract from the courage of the crewmen who took refugees on board under the noses of the Gestapo, crossed waters where the possibility of hitting a mine or being intercepted by a hostile vessel seemed very real, and returned to Danish harbors where—as the captured Snekkersten fisherman discovered early in the rescue—the Gestapo might well be waiting to arrest them.

For those who sought to reach freedom on lesser boats, the situation at sea was far more perilous. At least twenty-two Jews are known to have drowned when their escape boats capsized or sank. Two mass drownings, accounting for eleven deaths, occurred when two rowboats carrying a total of nineteen people overturned in the waves—one boat that had set out on the night of October 5 and another on October 7. The second of these boats carried the doomed Bruno, the boy who had evaded capture at the Gilleleje church one day earlier. Another seven refugees drowned on the night of October 9 when a fishing boat taking them to Sweden, very likely traveling with its navigation lights turned off to avoid detection, was accidentally rammed and sunk by a Swedish navy vessel. The Swedish navy vessel, ironically, was at sea to assist Jews trying to reach Sweden.

The actual death toll at sea is almost certainly higher than the twenty-two documented cases. Some Jews, it has been noted, took off on their own, individually or in small groups, "without knowing enough about conditions on the water in those cold windy October days."[94] They left without anything to document their departure, and could easily have disappeared without a trace.

Cold, windy days were nothing new to *Gerda III*'s crew, and the boat was built to take almost anything that nature was likely to dish out. The dangers that the Nazis presented to the boat and crew during the October rescue was another matter. As to that, *Gerda III* and the rest of the boats that took part in the evacuation had a number of things in their favor—some known and others unknown at the time.

The first and most significant factor was the number of Danes who threw themselves into the rescue effort and into the simultaneous surge in sabotage activity. The "intensified sabotage campaign" that the *New York Times* characterized as a "military answer to Germany's attempted purge of the Jews in Denmark" diverted Nazi forces from hunting Jews to preserving the Nazi supply chain. And the extraordinary number of people who instantly came forward to warn the Jews, to find temporary shelter for them in Denmark, and to transport them to the hundreds of rescue boats waiting in harbors and off beaches all along the Danish coast, overwhelmed the forces arrayed against them.

The rescue fleet also had a significant ally beneath the surface: herring. October is the peak of the herring season, and fishing boats left Zealand harbors day and night to catch them. In 1943, 1,300 fishing boats were licensed to operate from seventy harbors on the shores of Zealand and nearby Danish islands.[95] The Nazis banned pleasure boats from the Øresund when the rescue effort began, but interfering with the herring catch was unthinkable. For Nazi patrol boats at sea, the task was not simply spotting a fishing boat (or a similarly built boat such as *Gerda III*) but guessing which of the thousand boats to choose from were carrying refugees instead of fish.

The hazards at sea were also decreased by actions that limited the number of Nazi vessels patrolling the Øresund and by glimmers of humanity on the part of some German naval officers who were on patrol.

The Danes took the first action that smoothed the way for the seaborne rescue when they scuttled their naval vessels at the Royal Dockyards, or took them to Sweden, rather than let them fall into Nazi hands. That action deprived the Nazis of additional coastal vessels that might have made a more effective blockade. The episode, however, was not entirely encouraging. The Nazis' ability to prevent several Danish warships from reaching Sweden—by strafing them from the air or intercepting them with more powerful German warships—must have worried rescuers who set out to make the same crossing in wooden work boats.

Contemporary reports establish that the German navy maintained a robust presence on the Øresund throughout the rescue. For the larger German vessels, however, the principal tasks were securing the Baltic against intrusions by Allied warships and safeguarding the flow of iron ore and other materials from Norway. Smaller patrol boats, of a type more suitable for boarding fishing boats and other potential rescue craft, posed a greater danger to *Gerda III*. At the critical moment, however, the number of patrol boats in operation was reduced by the decisions of two German naval officers in Denmark.

One of these decisions was purely fortuitous. A squadron of six German patrol boats, based twenty-four miles north of Copenhagen in Helsingør, was temporarily confined to port as a result of the district commander's order reassigning their crews to minesweepers. The crews were reassigned just as the rescue was getting underway.

The second decision, Georg Duckwitz wrote in his memoirs, was a deliberate effort to facilitate the evacuation of the Jews. Another squadron of patrol boats, based in Copenhagen, was under the command of Corvettenkapitan Richard Camman. Duckwitz wrote in his memoirs that he paid a visit to Camman—the final step in his efforts to save Denmark's Jews—right after he told Hans Hedtoft what was about to unfold.

Camman was a decorated World War I naval officer. Between the wars, Camman rose to the top ranks of Germany's merchant marine, becoming the captain of a Hamburg-Amerika Line ocean liner. Duckwitz, who had been Hamburg-Amerika's agent in New York, befriended Camman and hoped that he would share Duckwitz's disgust with the plan to send Denmark's Jews to the concentration camps. Given what Duckwitz asked Camman to do, Duckwitz's life may well have depended on it.

Duckwitz told Camman what was about to befall the Jews and what was needed to facilitate their escape. Following that meeting, Camman ordered his patrol boats taken out of service for "repairs," an order that kept many of them in port during the early days of the rescue effort. Duckwitz later wrote in his memoirs that Camman "saw to it that the coast guard ships [based in Copenhagen] were taken out of action. He took a great personal risk but he did so without hesitation."[96]

By the time Camman's patrol boats returned to active duty—his ruse could only last so long—many Jews had crossed from Denmark to Sweden. The fate of those who remained, and of the Danish mariners who were determined to save them, was now largely in the hands of the German officers who commanded Camman's boats. In some cases, their conscience triumphed over Nazi policy. One German officer's moment of truth was described by a refugee, Ulrik Plesner, who was crossing the Øresund in the hold of his neighbor's fishing boat when it was stopped by a German patrol boat. He wrote in an Israeli newspaper twenty-five years later:

> On a dark and rough night, my neighbor sailed with lights out and the fish hold full of Danish Jews. He was caught in the search light of a German Navy patrol boat

which ordered him to stop and kept him covered. The German captain shouted: "What are you carrying?" and Ole shouted back "fish." The captain then jumped onto the deck, leaving his crew to cover him, and demanded that the hatches to the fish hold be removed. He stared a long time at several dozen frightened people looking up at him. Finally, he turned to Ole, in a loud voice that could be heard by his own crew as well: "Ah fish!" Then he returned to his boat and sailed into the night.[97]

No crew member or passenger on any of the rescue boats could have counted on that decision. It is likely that the German officer could not have forecast his own decision—that it was something he wrestled with during the "long time" that he stared down into the hold at the people whose fate he controlled. In another occupied country, without the moral example of a population that rose up to save the Jews, he may have made a different choice.

Gerda III might have encountered the same officer, or one of a similar mindset, on the occasions when it was followed and hailed by German patrol boats. Or perhaps *Gerda III*'s crew simply convinced the German crews that the boat was carrying nothing but supplies for the Lighthouse and Buoy Service, supplies they in fact delivered after they had put the Jews safely ashore in Sweden. It was impossible to know the outcome of any such encounter in advance, and it was difficult to know what made for a peaceful parting when it was over. All that could be known was that every such encounter carried the potential for disaster.

Gerda III's crewmen continued to flirt with disaster after the Jewish rescue operation was completed. The Nazi attack on Denmark's Jews was a turning point for them, as it was for Henny and her associates on land. In the coming months, members of the crew, and the Lighthouse and Buoy Service as a whole, moved beyond humanitarian activities to perform ever more dangerous roles for the armed resistance.

Chapter Six

FROM RESCUE TO RESISTANCE

AT THE START OF THE RESCUE EFFORT, Jørgen Kieler was trying to transform his student group from paper warriors, who defied the Nazis by reporting and advocating resistance activities in an underground newspaper, to full participants in the armed revolt. Kieler wanted to become a saboteur and bring the group along with him. It was not a decision that he took lightly or made in haste. It was a decision that he and members of his group had wrestled with for at least eight months before resolving to take up arms. The Nazis' attempt to send Denmark's Jews to the concentration camps, and the month-long effort by Kieler's group to thwart that atrocity, provided the final impetus that they needed.

Kieler's desire took root on January 27, 1943, when Britain's Royal Air Force (the "RAF") staged an unsuccessful bombing raid on the Burmeister & Wain shipyard in Copenhagen, a facility that the Nazis had taken over to build and repair German warships.[98] Most of the bombs missed the shipyard and fell on surrounding homes and businesses. A strong moral urge to fight the Nazis had already been welling up within Kieler before those bombs fell. But Kieler saw the collateral damage caused by the RAF's bombing of Burmeister & Wain—coupled with the absence of major damage to the target itself—as strong additional reasons for Danes to take matters into their own hands. Only precisely placed explosives on

the ground could both ensure destruction of the intended targets—
striking a blow to the Nazi war machine—and protect Danish lives
and property from the unintended effects of aerial bombardment.
Reflecting his own conviction, Kieler boldly proclaimed in his
underground newspaper in the spring of 1943 that "it has now
become clear that the Danish nation recognized the validity of
sabotage as a weapon against the Germans."[99]

While Kieler was ready to enter the armed resistance in the
spring of 1943, two factors held him back prior to October. First,
what he proclaimed to be clear to the Danish nation was not yet clear
to every member of his group. Some members (including his sister
Elsebet) had moral qualms about taking up arms—until the Nazi
attack on the Jews erased all such reservations. Second, Kieler and
his band of university students were untrained and unequipped for
armed resistance. The solution to that problem began to take shape
in September 1943, when his cousin Sven Kieler paid an unexpected
visit to Jørgen at his Copenhagen apartment.

Sven, part of the crew that scuttled the patrol boat *Polar Bear*, was
captured and interned with other cadets from August 29 through
early October. But, after weeks of total confinement at the Royal
Dockyards, cadets were granted a small measure of freedom. In
another failed effort to cool the anti-Nazi fervor that was sweeping
Denmark, the Nazis offered cadets a limited number of passes to visit
family members up to one day per week. With authentic passes to
work from, the cadets began forging additional passes for resistance
work. In September, a few weeks after his internment began, Sven
used one such pass to make his way to Jørgen's apartment. Upon
his arrival, he asked Jørgen if he could use the apartment "to store
a number of weapons that [Sven] and his friends were going to
smuggle from [the Royal Dockyards at] Holmen."[100] Jørgen agreed,
on the condition that his group could also use the weapons for "the
resistance struggle." The deal was struck.

Sven returned a short time later with Mix, who "began to
smuggle light arms along with Sven."[101] In the ensuing weeks, Mix

was a regular visitor to Jørgen's apartment, amassing a cache of weapons that he had smuggled past the Dockyard gates.

Mix also recruited new members from the cadet ranks, people who brought at least rudimentary knowledge of weapons and explosives. As Jørgen put it, we received "important support" for the sabotage group when, "via Sven Kieler and Mix, we made contact with a group of interned naval cadets who were keen to join the resistance."[102] Nine navy cadets, in addition to Sven and Mix, joined Kieler's group when the Nazis released them from the last vestiges of captivity in mid-October.

Finally, Mix brought *Gerda III*, its crew, and Henny into the fold.

Henny recounted that Mix "had become good friends with the lighthouse workers and the crew of *Gerda III*" during the eight days that he was held captive at the Drogden Lighthouse. His friendship with *Gerda III*'s crew continued to develop during the weeks that he was interned at the navy base where the boat docked outside the Lighthouse and Buoy Service's headquarters. Mix took care to learn "their point of view" about the war and the resistance, and found that it matched his own.[103] Mix's interest in the crew's thinking was understandable. For a naval cadet who was in the process of assembling material and personnel for a resistance group, *Gerda III*'s usefulness would have been too clear to overlook.

Mix also observed Henny going to and from the Lighthouse and Buoy Service's base at the Royal Dockyards, and he envisioned a role for her in his resistance plans. He learned from the crew that Henny "could be trusted" and that he could "fully confide in her"— which he did.

Mix approached Henny "sometime in the beginning of October" as she recalled it, well aware of the role she was performing in the Jewish rescue operation. Quite invisibly to Henny, he had contributed to her success by bringing *Gerda III* to Kieler's attention and melding it into Kieler's operation. Completing the rescue was still the top priority when they met, but Mix went straight to a discussion of "some *more* work" that he had in mind. Mix made it clear that "more work" meant armed resistance—sabotage above all else. Henny was startled by how directly he got to the point at this, their first meeting. Sabotage was not a subject that people raised with anyone on their first encounter, and generally didn't speak of at all. But it was clear to Henny that Mix had done his homework, vetting her with the *Gerda III* crew and relying on her conduct in the rescue operation to confirm the crew's high opinion of her. He knew what he was doing.

Henny wrote:

> For a long time we walked and talked together, and he told me a little about what the work was going to be about.... Mix did not hide that the work was dangerous and suggested that I take my time giving him an answer. There was no reason for me to wait because of course I wanted to join.[104]

Mix made a powerful impression on Henny, as he had on Jørgen. To Jørgen, Mix "left no doubt that he was the leader type."[105] Jørgen added that he "had great confidence in [Mix] right from the start and knew that we would soon become good friends." To Henny, Mix was "a young, dynamic navy cadet" who would soon become much more than a good friend.[106] Henny also noted that "everything he undertook had to go fast."

With Mix to vouch for her, and Kieler's first-hand assessment of the courage and competence that Henny brought to the rescue operation, Henny entered the inner circle of Kieler's armed resistance group. She began to "participate in meetings at [Kieler's] Raadhuisstraede [apartment]…and other places where we met up," to plan and prepare for the sabotage work to come.[107]

At the same time, and in a similar fashion, Kieler had proven himself to Mogens Staffeldt's core group. By doing so during the Jewish rescue operation, Kieler formed other important relationships that would vault his group into the forefront of the armed resistance.

Well before the Jewish rescue operation was concluded, Staffeldt had already expanded the activities that took place in the back of his bookstore beyond underground publishing and rescue work, making it an early center of the armed revolt. He was joined in these endeavors, and in the operation of his rescue network, by his younger brother Jørgen and by Jens Lillelund, soon to be known in the resistance by the code name "Finn." Finn was one of the two Holger Danske leaders who, in August 1943, planted and detonated the bombs that blew up the Forum. By early October, the Staffeldt brothers and Finn were joined by Svend Otto Nielsen, code named "John." Together, they would turn the back of Staffeldt's bookstore into a coordination and command center for the Danish resistance. The space from which Staffeldt's group directed hundreds of Jews to rescue boats became a place, in the words of British historian Harold Flanders, from which "saboteurs were sent out to blow up factories, disrupt rail and communications [networks], and liquidate traitors and informers."[108] Kieler, Mix, and Henny would be among those undertaking the missions.

In mid-October, just as Kieler's group was strengthened by the arrival of the newly freed cadets, Finn approached Kieler with a proposal. The Nazis had decimated Finn's Holger Danske group following its attack on the Forum. Its leader was seriously wounded and had to be evacuated to Sweden; many of its most active members followed him into exile. Finn now drew upon the people he came to know and trust during the Jewish rescue operation to reinvigorate Holger Danske. He proposed that Kieler's group join forces with them and operate under the name Holger Danske 2 (HD2). Kieler accepted.

A few days after Kieler agreed to merge his group into the Holger Danske organization, Finn returned to Kieler's apartment with Nielsen, a.k.a., John. John, who was another experienced saboteur, became one of HD2's principal leaders during its first few months of operation.

Finn also introduced Kieler to Jens Peter. This introduction was a product of Finn's contacts with Britain's Special Operations

Executive (the "SOE"). The SOE carried out sabotage and espionage missions in occupied Europe, directly where necessary and through local resistance groups where possible. The SOE trained Jens in England and then parachuted him back into Denmark to instruct Danish resistance leaders. Kieler described their first meeting:

> Along with Mix, I met Jens Peter…. Out of his bag he pulled detonators, fuses, ignition equipment, wads, plus various types of bombs and explosives. This was spread out on the table and so the lesson began.[109]

The SOE, using Finn and the Staffeldts to communicate target lists, would make good use of the training that it provided to Kieler and Mix.

While Kieler and Mix were being trained in "bombs and explosives," Mix gave Henny the training he felt she needed. Henny recounted:

> Before I became involved in any actions Mix thought it would be a good idea if I learned a little about weapons. One day we therefore [went to] Grib Forest…. [W]hen we got far enough into the woods, Mix took a machine gun and other smaller guns out of the box and started teaching me how to use such awful things.[110]

By the end of October 1943, HD2 had gelled, with a core group made up of Kieler and seven other members of his original university group (including his brother Flemming and sisters Elsebet and Bente), Mix, Sven, and nine fellow naval cadets, plus John and Henny. Kieler wrote that HD2 "included four women who were fully aware of the fact that the death penalty awaited anyone who accommodated or otherwise helped saboteurs."[111] Reflecting their deepening relationship, Kieler noted that one of those women was "Mix's girlfriend Henny."

Henny plainly "accommodated" and "helped" the men who planted the bombs. Describing the start of her work with HD2, Henny told her 1994 interviewer:

> My job was…among other things to help the boys before a sabotage [mission] to see if Germans were there. I usually walked with one of the boys and we were supposed to look very much in love, not caring about anything in the world except the two of us and at the same time look around to see if there were any Germans. That is how I got into it, and then one thing led to another.[112]

Kieler's memoirs and Henny's own accounts establish that she stored weapons, set up safe houses for the saboteurs, engaged in surveillance operations, and more. While her role in many of HD2's operations can only be inferred from her training and her partial "job" description, her daring roles in other operations have been preserved in exquisite detail.

As for *Gerda III*, at least one important role, the ongoing role of a lifeboat for resistance members and other Nazi targets, is well established. There are strong indications that it did more—that it also smuggled weapons and other supplies to Holger Danske and to other resistance fighters who continued the battle on Danish soil.

In organizing as Holger Danske 2, a part of the larger Holger Danske resistance network, Kieler took on an apt name. In Danish folklore, Holger Danske (Holger the Dane in English) was a hero who awoke in Kronborg Castle, of Hamlet fame, to defend Denmark in times of trouble. Now, with the addition of Kieler's group and others who proved themselves during the Jewish rescue operation, the Holger Danske organization was reawakening to oust Denmark's invaders.

One of the others who joined the ranks of Holger Danske was Christian Kisling, who used the vehicles at his ambulances and fire station to bring Jews hidden at Bispebjerg Hospital and other medical facilities to rescue boats. Over time, Kisling became the head of another Holger Danske unit and, by war's end, the head of all of Holger Danske. He spoke of the awakening succinctly and eloquently:

> At first public opinion was against sabotage, but then once the Germans started in with the Jews, and we had to help them escape, we got a taste of what it was like to fight the Germans and we liked it. We thought, now that the Jews are safe in Sweden, lets continue, let's go all the way.[113]

Kieler, Henny, and the other members of Holger Danske 2, had precisely the same thought as they embarked on their sabotage missions.

Holger Danske 2

HD2's first major target, designated by the SOE, was a factory that made radios and radio-jamming equipment for the Nazis. On November 9, 1943, two groups of HD2 operatives, a bomb unit, and four men armed with pistols, approached the plant. The bomb unit rushed toward the factory, tossed twenty-two pounds of explosives and several incendiary devices through the windows, and ran off. The weapons unit covered their escape, exchanging fire with the plant's guards. The building went up in flames as the saboteurs ran off into the darkness.

Over the next two weeks, HD2 carried out eight more missions using tactics and materials much like they used on the first mission. Then they stepped up their game.

At an industrial complex in the northern part of Copenhagen, the Hellerup Company manufactured sound locators that pinpointed Allied aircraft for German anti-aircraft batteries.

The locators made the skies over Denmark, where 1,300 British airmen were killed on the way to or from bombing targets in Germany, even more lethal. At the end of November, with another batch of locators about to be shipped, destroying Hellerup and its inventory became one of the SOE's top priorities.

John, Mix, and Jørgen staked out the factory, and they could not have been encouraged by what they saw. The factory space occupied the western portion of a large building; the eastern portion was occupied by the Danish and German harbor police. Three German guards with submachine guns were stationed near the entrance at the western end of the building. A long northern wall had a row of ground floor windows that the saboteurs could throw bombs through if they could get close enough. But there was no way to get there without scaling a fence and crossing an open field that was lit with searchlights from dusk to dawn—a field in which the saboteurs would come under fire long before they reached the building. There was also a second-floor row of windows that was of no use to the saboteurs but provided firing positions for any guards inside the building. The mission required more explosives, more weapons, and more risk than anything HD2 had attempted before. Despite the extreme danger, they decided to go forward.

Their plan called for three units: an eight-man bomb unit (including Mix and Jørgen), a four-man weapons unit (including John), and a third unit that was formed to break into a nearby electrical center and cut the power to the searchlights. The bomb and weapons units were to leap into action as soon as the lights went out.

On the night of the raid, November 28, the bomb unit waited in a cold rain for the chance to scale the fence and run to the ground floor windows with their explosives. They were divided into four two-man teams, each team carrying a British incendiary device and a homemade bomb containing thirty pounds of dynamite. When their team members cut the power to the searchlights, and the field ahead of them went dark, the bomb unit went into action. The bomb teams were only a third of the way across the field when guards opened fire on them from the second floor.

The weapons unit returned fire with submachine guns and pistols, allowing the bomb teams to reach their destinations. They managed to light the rain-soaked fuses, throw the bombs through the windows, and begin their retreat. Three of the four bombs went off as the saboteurs made their escape, severely damaging the building and destroying sixteen locators that were ready to be shipped the next day. Miraculously, everybody survived.

Jørgen described the raid as a turning point that "marked the start of a new course, a new spirit."

> Submachine guns were now part and parcel of each operation, which meant tougher fighting, a greater risk for us, but also the opportunity to carry out larger scale operations.... Earlier actions had gone out from the following premise: the maximum result without a loss of life. This had now changed to: the maximum result, even if lives are lost. Earlier on guile and surprise had been the tactics. Now it was more of an open fight, a military-style operation.[114]

Jørgen also described the operation as "the icing on the cake of John's career as a saboteur."[115]

EIGHT DAYS LATER, on December 8, John and Finn met to discuss future missions. Then they went to spend the night at the home of a seamstress, Hedvig Delbo, who had reportedly been "keen to establish contact with the Resistance."[116] She served them dinner, gave them a guest room, and then (as was later determined), called the Gestapo. As John and Finn bicycled away the next morning, they were followed by two cars loaded with Gestapo agents. A short chase ended in a gunfight. Finn escaped in the melee. John was shot seven times while managing to kill one Gestapo agent and wound another. He was taken away, still breathing, for interrogation by the Gestapo.

The members of HD2 had good reason to believe that Delbo had informed on John and Finn. To verify their suspicions, Finn called Delbo soon after he had contacted the others—ostensibly to tell her what had happened and to ask if he could come by for a farewell visit before he escaped to Sweden. At the appointed time, Kieler sent a "courting couple"—almost certainly Henny and Mix—to stroll by Delbo's house and watch for any reaction. The arrival of a Gestapo car at each end of her street confirmed that Delbo was an informer, and that she had to be killed.

As Kieler described it, "this was not a matter of revenge or punishment but of self-preservation."[117] Delbo had evidently won the confidence of John and Finn and may have learned enough from them to endanger the whole HD2 organization. A plan was set in motion to kill her the next day.

The plan was thorough, perhaps too much so. Finn would enter Delbo's apartment and shoot her. To assure that Delbo was home, and that Gestapo agents were not with her, Henny would enter her apartment first, on the pretext of wanting a dress made, while Finn waited in an adjacent hallway. Mix and fourteen other men would deploy around Delbo's home to cover Finn's and Henny's escape. They would leap into action if the Gestapo returned before Finn and Henny could get out of the building. Everything began according to plan. Henny wrote of the day:

> I was to go up to Mrs. Delbo's apartment...to see if she was home and if there were any Germans guarding her. As she was a seamstress, it would be very natural if I brought her a piece of fabric and asked her to take measurements for a dress for me....
>
> I rang the doorbell at Mrs. Delbo's and she came out and asked me to come inside.
>
> The doors to the kitchen and living room were opened and apparently there were no Germans. But another customer was there trying on a dress. She took forever and finally I did not dare wait any longer. Finn was outside waiting, so I told Mrs. Delbo that I would return again the next day. Then I ran over to Finn, who was nervously pacing the hallway.... [Finn] insisted on waiting until we

had seen the customer leave the apartment. We waited and waited and nobody left....[118]

On the streets around Delbo's apartment, Mix and the other members of the assassination team also waited. Eventually they attracted attention. Police arrested Mix and one of his comrades and took them to the police station for questioning. When the police arrived, Henny later wrote, "Finn ran up a couple of stairs" while Henny "left very quietly and calmly down Faxegade," the street on which Delbo lived, "and was gone."

Finn returned to Delbo's apartment that night. As he related it to Kieler:

A Norwegian woman came to the door, closely followed by Mrs. Delbo. When [Delbo] saw Finn she let out a scream and fled into the flat. Finn shot her with his silenced pistol....[119]

Finn left thinking he had gotten the job done. Not until the next day did he and the other members of HD2 learn that Delbo survived the gunshot and was telling the Gestapo about the attempt on her life. The certainty that the Gestapo would make Finn one of its most wanted men endangered more than his life. Finn's knowledge of the SOE and the entire Holger Danske organization meant that his capture and the brutal interrogation that was sure to follow would put much of the resistance movement at risk. Finn and his family were therefore hidden in Denmark for the next twelve days. On December 22, they were taken across the Øresund to Sweden.

Delbo also went into hiding—until another Holger Danske group found and killed her on March 9, 1944.

The evacuation of Finn and his family demonstrates why the number of resistance people taken across the Øresund was so high—hundreds on *Gerda III* alone. It was rarely enough to evacuate just one person. In Finn's case, it was determined that transporting Finn and his family would suffice. Had it been known that John was still alive, being interrogated and tortured by the Nazis, the decision might well have been made to evacuate the entire HD2 group—an action that was later ordered for the survivors of its final sabotage mission. Until then, Henny had to wonder whether Delbo and the Gestapo had figured out the real reason for her visit. And all of HD2 had to ponder the consequences of failing to carry out the killing they had attempted as a "matter of self-preservation."

At the same time, other events drove home the perils faced by rescuers as well as armed resisters. On December 10, two days after the Gestapo shot and captured John, Gestapo agents killed Cato Bakman, the medical student who had helped arrange passage on *Gerda III* for Jews hidden at Bispebjerg Hospital. Bakman had not made the transition to sabotage work—his moral objection to taking up arms prevented him from doing so—but he continued to risk his life as a rescuer. Together with Doctor Køster, he carried on the work of arranging passage on the dwindling number of boats that still dared to make covert crossings—*Gerda III* among them— to save resistance fighters, Allied airmen, and any Jews who failed to escape during October. On the night of December 10, Bakman went to Dr. Køster's apartment to continue their work. Bakman was waiting for Dr, Køster to return when six Gestapo agents—pursuing both Køster and Bakman—came through the door. Bakman made a dash to the window and jumped to the ground two stories below. The Gestapo shot him in the back as he tried to limp away. Mortally wounded, he was carried to the Bispebjerg emergency room, where he died in the arms of a nurse he had married only a few weeks earlier.[120]

THE MEMBERS OF HD2 had no time to mourn Bakman or to worry about the ramifications of their failed assassination attempt. Within a day after the attempted Delbo assassination, and Bakman's death, Kieler received a request to carry out a mission in Jutland. The SOE had made the Varde Steelworks on the west coast of Jutland a high priority target. A local sabotage group that was tapped for the operation backed out after the Gestapo arrested two of its members. Kieler agreed to fill the void. On December 11, Kieler and seven other HD2 saboteurs boarded a ferry to Jutland and proceeded to Varde. That night, they gathered at the home of the Chief Constable, a member of the resistance, to review drawings and plans that were prepared for the attack. The plan was refined over a 1:00 a.m. serving of sandwiches and coffee. Then it was put into motion. Eight bombs made of plastic explosives ripped the steel plant apart and put it out of commission for six months. The December 13, 1943 edition of the *New York Times* ran an account of HD2's raid under the headline, "Danes Blow up Plant Making German Arms, Armed Patriots Overpower Guards at Varde Steel Works."[121]

HD2 carried out another three successful missions, in rapid succession, before leaving Jutland and returning to Copenhagen. When they returned, they set their sights on Burmeister & Wain, the target of the failed RAF raid that began Kieler's transformation from an underground publisher to a saboteur one year earlier. Having survived the RAF raid, and more recent attacks by other sabotage groups, Burmeister & Wain continued to produce equipment used by German submarines and surface warships.

BURMEISTER & WAIN was both a shipbuilder and a leading producer of marine diesel engines. HD2 targeted the facility where the company manufactured and repaired engines, propellers, and other propulsion gear. That waterfront facility was located where the southern end of the Christianshavn Canal meets Copenhagen harbor, a little less than half a mile from where Henny berthed *Gerda III* during the rescue operation. The plan for attacking Burmeister & Wain also required a boat, but this time *Gerda III* did not fit the bill. The boat used in the attack would have to be abandoned near the scene of the crime. *Gerda III* was too valuable for that, and leaving it behind would link Henny and her family to the attack. It was plainly preferable to "borrow" a different boat from an unknown owner.

Kieler described the Burmeister & Wain operation as "more ambitious and daring" than any of HD2's twenty-two prior operations. It was certainly more complex. The plan called for Kieler and three other men to "borrow" a sailboat they picked out for the mission and sail it to a place where they would rendezvous with a Danish police boat. The police boat would then tow them to a wharf near the target where ten more men, led by Mix, would be waiting. Kieler and his three-man crew would be lightly armed with pistols. Mix and his ten men were another story. They would be waiting with submachine guns, hand grenades, and hundreds of pounds of explosives. When Kieler arrived, Mix's contingent would board the sailboat with their equipment. The combined team would then proceed quietly down the Christianshavn side of the harbor, under the Knippelsbro Bridge that connected Christianshavn with Copenhagen, to Burmeister & Wain's wharf. They would climb ashore, overpower the guards, plant the bombs, and escape on the same boat they arrived in. The escape route would take them further down the Chistianshavn side of the harbor to the Langebro Bridge. From there most of the crew would cross the bridge on foot and disappear into the crowds of Copenhagen, while Mix and a few other saboteurs would load the weapons and remaining grenades in suitcases and take them to waiting cars. Mix and his contingent would then drive through Christianshavn to a street where Henny would be waiting, ready to lead them to a hiding place that she had arranged.

The operation took place on January 15, 1944, a Saturday when there would be no workers in the facility. Kieler and his team cut the sailboat loose from its berth around 6:00 p.m. and were on time for their 7:00 p.m. rendezvous with the Danish police boat. It was past seven when a craft that appeared to be the Danish police boat came into view, and Kieler signaled it. But the Danish police boat was still at its dock, where its commander was trying to convince his nervous subordinate to go forward with the mission. The boat that Kieler mistakenly hailed was a German harbor patrol boat crewed by German marines. As the boat came into sharper focus, Kieler and his team threw their pistols overboard and prepared for the worst. Lacking any good explanation for why they were out at night in a boat they didn't own, the marines arrested them and brought them to a German ship to be interrogated. While they awaited the arrival of an interrogation team, the German harbor patrol boat remained alongside the larger vessel. Sidelining the patrol boat was an unintended benefit of Kieler's error. With the patrol boat out of action, there was one less risk for Mix and the other participants—if they could find a replacement for Kieler's sailboat and salvage the mission.

The Danish police boat eventually got underway. When the crew found no one at the first rendezvous point, they proceeded to the berth where Mix's team was waiting. Mix, Kieler later wrote, "showed his characteristic talent for leadership."[122] With no sailboat to take the saboteurs to the target, Mix convinced the Danish police to step ashore and lend their boat to his team. Mix's team was running late, they were shorthanded, and their escape plans were in jeopardy. But they had too much going for them to abort the mission. Mix wrote of his group:

> We were incredibly well armed. Everyone had a pistol and there were twelve submachine guns available as well, plus masses of hand grenades. We were determined to carry out the mission against all odds.[123]

They had plenty of explosive power as well—seven bombs containing 412 pounds of dynamite. Mix revised each person's assignment as they motored to the target in the borrowed police boat.

> While we were underway we re-allotted the tasks…. There was a lot to do and now nearly a third of our forces was not present. Well, everything turned out OK. We landed and the guards were held up as planned—some armed, some unarmed….[124]

When Mix determined that they had stayed at the target as long as they dared, he gave the signal to "get to the boats—ignite the bombs where they are." When all ten men were back on board the police boat, Mix returned to their starting point. He wrote:

> The course of the retreat had been altered. We had to take the police boat back to safety again. When we got to the Knippelsbro Bridge we heard the first explosion and then a further five in quick succession. This meant that one bomb had failed to go off....[125]

Six bombs were enough to knock the plant out of commission for three to four months.

Henny was waiting elsewhere in Christianshavn, near a room that her father rented for her older sister. The room was on the top floor of a building next to Henny's home and a navy enclave known as the Søkvaesthuset. Henny wrote in her account of the Burmeister & Wain operation that the room "was not the ideal location to store the stuff being used to sabotage" the plant but "having no alternative it was decided to use [it] anyway." To keep her sister out of the room on the night of the raid, Henny told her that she "was having a boyfriend visit"—which was at least partially true—and asked her to stay with a girlfriend.[126]

Henny left her parents' home at about 5:00 p.m. and "walked around the streets of Christianshavn" to pass the time, but time seemed to stand still. She looked at her watch constantly, waiting for the moment when the bombs were to go off. When the moment came, there was nothing to relieve the strain, nothing to signal that the plan had worked and that Mix was on his way to her. Then, well past the agreed upon time, she heard the first explosion, followed, as she recalled it, "by at least five others."

As the explosions reverberated through Christianshavn, people left their homes and gathered around Henny in small groups. Their eyes turned to the sky above Burmeister & Wain—to what Henny later described as a purple sky set aglow by flames and rising embers.

Only Henny's eyes remained fixed at street level, riveted on Mix's escape route. In her words:

> Now I knew that the boys must have left Burmeister and that Mix and a couple of others must be on their way towards Overgaden [the street on which Henny's home and her sister's room were located] with all their gear. They were supposed to arrive by car, which was to stop a short distance from Søkvaesthuset where I was to meet them so we could proceed together up to the room.
>
> Time went by, the car did not arrive. Now I was really afraid.... Suddenly [I] spotted Mix, Filler, Reib and Stig further down the street, walking with some very large and heavy suitcases.... The boys pulled up their collars in order not to be recognized and in the general confusion we [managed to get] all the way up to the attic room without anybody noticing us.... Filler, Reib and Stig got out of Søkvaesthuset without any problems.... Mix and I pulled all the furniture out in front of the door..., then we put the suitcases [loaded with guns and grenades] on the floor and spent a very horrible night on top of the suitcases.[127]

Kieler and those arrested with him spent only eight days in captivity. Having been in German custody when the sabotage mission was carried out, they had the ultimate alibi as far as that was concerned. The only charge they faced was boat theft, for which the Germans turned them over to Danish authorities who had no interest in holding them any further. "So was the end of one of our most successful operations," Kieler wrote. "What actually happened was not discovered until some weeks later by the Gestapo, but by that time the participants in the operation were either already facing a death sentence or had fled to Sweden."[128]

THE MEMBERS OF HD2 had a little less than three weeks to enjoy their success before their final venture. It began on February 3 with another call to undertake a mission in Varde. With the resistance group in Varde still short of manpower, HD2 was asked to play the lead role in an attack on two adjacent factories just north of the German border. The Callesen and Hamag factories in Aabenraa, both SOE designated targets, were unquestionably important. One supplied the Nazis with equipment for U-boats and the other with equipment for warplanes. But the mission could hardly have been less promising. Many of the locals in this border region had strong ties to Germany and were more closely allied with the occupation than the resistance. It would be hard to get about the small town without being noticed. For HD2 members, who brought no cars and were unfamiliar with the territory, it would be hard to move around at all. After the raid, there would be few escape routes and few places to hide. What escape routes did exist would be closely watched by German troops who were garrisoned nearby. All of that was known to Kieler when, after a brief meeting with resistance leaders in Varde, he summoned his forces to Aabenraa.

Fourteen HD2 saboteurs, including Kieler, arrived in Aabenraa on February 4. Individually and in small groups, they found their way to the home of an automobile mechanic named Koch who had been vouched for by the few resistance people in the region. They were joined there by Viggo Hansen, who participated in the attack on the Varde Steelworks and persuaded Kieler to sign on for this operation. Viggo brought plans, showing the layout of the factories, and twenty-seven plastic explosive devices.

Around midnight they proceeded to Aabenraa Castle, a gathering place close to the targets. A few local resistance members joined them, bringing the total number of attackers to eighteen. Six people were assigned to Hamag, the softer target. The other twelve, including Jørgen and his brother Flemming, took the harder target at Callesen. The saboteurs left in pairs and made their way to the plants.

The Hamag team completed their mission without difficulty. Five bombs, set to go off in thirty minutes, were inserted. As the team made its escape, the sound of explosions confirmed the success of the mission.

Callesen was HD2's downfall. The Callesen squad reached a locked entrance that was the only way inside the plant. As they arrived, they could hear guards on the other side of the door phoning for reinforcements. Jørgen shot the lock off with his submachine gun and led his contingent into the factory. They had just enough time to plant their twenty-two bombs, set the detonators, and leave. This time, there was no sound of success. German troops, alerted by the guards, arrived from nearby barracks in time to defuse the bombs, and only seconds too late to capture or kill the men who planted them.

Despite their narrow escape from the Callesen factory, Jørgen and his crew were hardly safe. It was 2:30 in the morning, and they had no vehicles to carry them away from the area. More importantly, they had no intention of leaving. Going into the mission, the plan had been to disperse and return home as soon as possible after the attacks. But, when it became clear that the Callesen attack had failed, Jørgen decided to attack again the next night, seeking to do with six remaining people what his team had been unable to do with twelve.

Jørgen and five other saboteurs (Viggo Hansen and Jens Jørgensen from Varde; Peer Borup, Klaus Rønholt, and Neils Hjorth from HD2) walked to Koch's home to wait until the most acute danger subsided. Because they had used all of their bombs in the first attempt, Jens tried to get back to Varde for a new batch of explosives. The Gestapo caught him at the local train station and shot him when he tried to escape. The remaining saboteurs at Koch's home, not knowing Jens' fate, awaited his return. Fearing that the Gestapo would pay Koch a visit, they hid in a tool shed behind his house.

When the Gestapo did arrive at Koch's home, led by a local informer, they did not overlook the tool shed. As the Gestapo agents pried the door open, a gunfight erupted.

The first casualty, Peer Borup, was shot and killed in the shed. Kieler later remembered Peer as an ardent participant in the rescue mission—a boyhood friend from Jutland who helped many Jews reach freedom on *Gerda III* and the fishing boats recruited by Ebba Lund.

Klaus, who had been a member of Jørgen's group since their underground press days—and who, accompanied by Kieler's sister, had raised a million Kroner for the rescue effort during the first weekend in October—was shot in the leg. When the fighters in the shed ran out of bullets, Klaus used his good leg to smash a window, and the four survivors managed to climb out and escape across a field into the woods. Jørgen and Klaus moved on together—Klaus leaving a trail of blood in the snow from the bullet wound in one leg and a gash in the other. Jørgen was carrying Klaus on his back when the Gestapo caught up with them and shot Jørgen in the neck. Jørgen and Klaus, seriously wounded but alive, were loaded onto the back of a German army truck and taken to a Gestapo prison.

Most of the other saboteurs fared better. Those who tried to get out made it. But two never tried. Flemming Kieler stayed in the area with Georg Jansen, another member of HD2. The next day, as Flemming and Georg tried to reunite with Jørgen, another informer put the Gestapo on their trail. They were reunited with Jørgen and Klaus in a Nazi prison, where the four HD2 members were brutally interrogated. They disclosed nothing under questioning. But Flemming disclosed just enough to a cell-mate, a Nazi collaborator masquerading as a sympathetic fellow prisoner, to enable the Gestapo to find and arrest his sisters, Elsebet and Bente.

AS THE GESTAPO worked its way through HD2's ranks, Jørgen Staffeldt, who had taken over Finn's role as the leader of the entire Holger Danske organization, ordered HD2's remaining members to go into hiding and await passage to Sweden. Henny heard the news from Mix. She wrote in 1980:

> It was now decided by the higher coordinating council that the remaining members of...HD2 should be transported to Sweden.... It was too risky allowing anyone who knew

too much about the illegal actions and the participants to
stay.... Furthermore, it would be better for our friends who
had been imprisoned by the Germans to know that all the
rest of the group had gotten away and were safe in Sweden.
Then they could reveal the names...if they were tortured
by the Gestapo. So there was no excuse and we had to give
in and the whole group went into hiding. This meant that
you were not allowed to stay in your own home....[129]

Throughout their months-long sabotage campaign, Henny
and the other members of HD2 attempted to live as normally as
possible between missions—going to class or work, living at home,
being seen by friends at the usual times and places—in the belief
that the veneer of normalcy was their best disguise. The technique
was viable until the first arrests. All that remained now was to go
underground without a trace, and to escape without leaving a trail
that could implicate others.

The members of HD2 who had been ordered to leave Denmark
were allowed one short visit to their homes to pick up a few belongings
and say their goodbyes. Henny returned to her family home on the
Christianshavn Canal and, for the first time, told her parents what
she had been doing in the months after the rescue—in the months
after her father warned her not to get too deeply involved. There
was, in her words, "not one reproach."

In a private conversation with her father, however, there was a
statement she instantly regretted, and a request for a promise she
could not make. Henny told her father that she had been given a
poison pill to take if the Nazis caught her before she could reach
Sweden. Paul Sinding tried to extract a promise that Henny would
not swallow the pill no matter what might happen, reciting the old
maxim "as long as there is life there is hope." Henny listened, but
gave no assurance.

Henny and her mother hugged and cried and then, as Henny
recalled it, her mother "hurried me on so that I could reach safety
on the other side of the Øresund." Henny stepped outside, crossed

over the Christianshavn Canal, and entered a life of hiding and exile, unsure what she would do with the pill she carried if the moment to use it arrived.

Mix, by now much in love with Henny, arranged to keep her safe in Copenhagen while he initiated the next steps in their escape to Sweden. As Henny related it, "Mix had borrowed an apartment in *Nyboder*," the navy housing area in Copenhagen where Henny began life, and instructed her to wait there until she could be evacuated. The Yellow Houses of *Nyboder* continued to be occupied by junior navy officers and sailors with whom Mix felt comfortable and whose help he enlisted to organize the escape for himself and Henny. Henny further noted that Mix "arranged for someone to stand guard so I should not feel alone at night—particularly after he had left."[130]

Ultimately a plan for evacuating Mix and Henny was put together by navy officers with whom Mix maintained contact during his resistance work. Although the Danish navy no longer had ships of its own, its officers had good contacts in the maritime community and could be relied upon to fill the void—insofar as the evacuation of Mix and his colleagues were concerned—left by the shootings, arrests, and hot pursuit of other HD2 members. As Henny put it, "the Navy was in charge of arranging our transports to Sweden, but they were somewhat slow in doing so."[131]

Mix's reliance on his fellow navy personnel to arrange their transportation to Sweden provides some explanation for why he and Henny did not attempt a quick escape on *Gerda III*. Turning to *Gerda III*, moreover, could have placed Henny, Mix, and others in even greater peril. If the Nazis already knew of Henny's connection to *Gerda III*, they could have kept a close watch on the boat while they tried to chase Mix and Henny down. And if the Nazis had not yet made that connection, attempting to escape on *Gerda III* might well have led the Nazis to the boat, with grave consequences for the crew and for their commanding officer—Henny's father. So, Henny put her faith in Mix and his navy colleagues and awaited their orders.

Mix's departure orders came first. On February 16—the day the Gestapo arrested Elsebet and Bente Kieler—Mix was told to be ready to depart within twenty-four hours. Henny, she and Mix were told, would be taken separately during one of the next few evenings. So, February 16 became a day for final preparations and goodbyes. Mix and Henny met on a Copenhagen street and walked to Mogens Staffeldt's bookstore for a parting conversation.

The Staffeldts were in the store when Mix and Henny arrived. After a few words, an employee told Jørgen Staffeldt that somebody wanted to see him behind the store. Jørgen asked Mix and Henny to wait as he stepped out the back door. Mogens followed a short time later. Gestapo agents arrested each of the Staffeldt brothers as they emerged.

When the Staffeldts failed to return within a few minutes, Henny and Mix realized that the Nazis had taken them. Knowing how close they had also come to being captured, and what danger they were still in, Henny and Mix ran from the store before the Gestapo returned to search for other Holger Danske members, weapons, and clues that could lead to the capture of other resistance fighters. Henny later learned that the Gestapo waited until the next morning to search the store, by which time the prizes that the Nazis were after had been removed in a daring operation. During the night, members of the resistance entered the store and "with the assistance of an ambulance operated by the brave driver Kisling," in Henny's words, emptied the basement storage room that "had been full of weapons and ammunition."[132] Kisling, Henny added, "often helped the resistance movement carry out tasks like these."

Although Henny and Mix evaded capture at the bookstore, it was a close call, and it demonstrated that the Gestapo was closing in. As Henny put it, she and Mix "were deeply shaken" by the events.[133] Mix continued to work on their evacuation and on assuring Henny's survival in the interim. Henny wrote:

> That same evening Mix and I said good bye to each other. I promised Mix that I would stay indoors...with my bodyguard until I was picked up for my transport....

Four days later, on the evening of February 20, Henny was driven nine miles north of Copenhagen to a Lyngby estate owned by Danish Jews who escaped to Sweden during the October rescue. When Henny arrived at the home, which was to be the jumping off point for her own escape to Sweden, she was elated to find three other HD2 members who would be joining her. Christian Friis-Hansens, one of the navy cadets who Mix had brought into HD2, was part of the group. The two others, Hanne ("Nan") Møller and her brother Hans Tellus Møller, had been members of Kieler's student group since its underground press days, and were active participants in HD2's rescue and resistance work. Three refugees from Estonia (two parents and their young daughter) completed the escape group.

Later that night, the group was driven to a dock where it had been arranged for a police boat, manned by crewmen already accustomed to making illegal crossings for the resistance, to take them on board. That night, however, there would be no escape. As Henny recounted, "there was a strong northeasterly storm" with "such high winds that the motorboat was unable to reach the shore."

Henny described what came next:

> We were taken back to the villa in Lyngby where we spent the rest of the night sleeping on the floor, the sofa or wherever possible. The next evening we were picked up and taken [six miles further north] to a house near Humlebaek Harbor and when it was dark we were ordered one by one to make our way down to the harbor where the police boat was docked. Nearby there was a German vessel with guards onboard.... [But] it was not until we were a ways out into the Øresund that we were observed and followed by a German patrol boat that fired some shots at us.[134]

The gunfire, and need to take evasive action for much of the eight and one-third mile crossing from Humlebaek to Raa, kept Henny and her shipmates in a precarious state. As Henny's escape boat raced across the Øresund, maintaining a high speed that might have been inadvisable were it not for the Germans shooting at them, the boat began to take on water. Accounts fail to specify whether the seawater came through a bullet hole, came over the rail as waves and spray engulfed the boat, or entered from both possible sources. What was clear is that water rose to dangerous levels in the engine compartment, threatening to bring the engine and the escape to an abrupt halt. It became Christian's job to throw his strength into the arduous task of operating a manual bilge pump, mounted inside the cabin where he and the other escaping passengers had been placed, at a fast enough clip to get water out of the boat as rapidly as it was coming in.

At the end of its dash across the Øresund, the police boat discharged its passengers in Sweden early on the morning of February 22. After establishing their identity and the reasons for their escape to the satisfaction of the local police, Henny and her companions were brought to a resettlement area. Through inquiries at that location, Henny confirmed that Mix had also made it to Sweden.

The horrors that Henny and Mix avoided by their escape were made plain by the fate of the Holger Danske members who did not get out. The Nazis subjected Jørgen Kieler, his brother Flemming, Klaus Ronholdt, and others who were captured after the Hamag and Callesen raids, to months of interrogations in Denmark. The Nazis then transported them to Porta Westphalica—a prison camp in Germany where resisters were forced into slave labor and where many were worked, starved, or beaten to death. In April, before the Nazis transferred him to Porta Westphalica, Jørgen was briefly reunited in a Copenhagen prison with John, the former Holger Danske leader who Gestapo agents had shot after Delbo alerted them to John's presence. The Nazis apparently hoped that, if Jørgen and John were placed together, they might be overheard saying things to each other that they would never knowingly disclose to the Nazis. When that did not work, John, already near death from his bullet wounds, was removed from his cell and executed by a Nazi firing squad. Jørgen, who had also been given a death sentence, was given something of a reprieve when, instead of facing a firing squad, he was sent to face the likelihood of a slower death at Porta Westphalica.

By contrast, Henny and Mix were beyond the Nazis' reach and, for the first time in nearly four years, in a place that seemed untouched by war. Henny was struck by the simple pleasures of living in a nation at peace: the absence of hostile forces at every turn; the freedom to walk well-lit streets at any hour, unrestrained by curfews and nightly black-outs; and stores that were well stocked with chocolates and other luxuries that were hard to find in wartime Denmark. But for Mix—as events in 1945 would demonstrate—safety and peace in another land were not enough.

As soon as he arrived in Sweden, Mix joined the Danish Brigade, an army in exile. The men of the Brigade trained in Växjö Sweden, not far from where Henny had come ashore, preparing to fight alongside the Allies to liberate Denmark in an invasion that never came. With no role for women at the Brigade's base, and no employment or lodging to be had in the rural area surrounding it, Henny found a job and a place to live in Stockholm, over two hundred miles away.

For months, Henny and Mix met only sporadically, on the rare occasions when Mix could get a pass to Stockholm or they could rendezvous near his base. But for the most part, as Henny recounted, they "lived on each other's letters."[135] Mix's letters were a combination of affection and, in a guarded fashion, bits of wartime intelligence that came his way. One such item in a March letter obliquely addressed the final act in the hunt for Mrs. Delbo, the seamstress turned informer who Henny and other HD2 members had attempted to assassinate. Never using Delbo's name or mentioning that she had been shot, Mix sardonically wrote that "it was sad...your seamstress should end up like this," adding: "I so wish I had been with her in her last moments. I might have comforted her."[136]

An Easter reunion in Stockholm, which lasted several days, raised both of their spirits until their mood was dampened by Mix's return to the base. A longer-term solution to their separation came later that spring when the Brigade's commanders began to recognize that some women—still very few in their estimation—were needed for supporting roles at the training base and in any operations that might follow in Denmark. Henny leapt at the opportunity to get closer to Mix and to any fighting that might come. With dogged persistence, Henny worked her way from a headquarters desk, to a field kitchen at Mix's base, to a firing range—a place where pistol, machine gun, and grenade practice supplemented the lessons she received from Mix back in Grib Forest.

The Danish Brigade housed Henny, with fourteen other female volunteers, in a dilapidated old house that was separated from the base by two miles of woods. The distance and terrain were intended to maintain strict decorum and limit socializing. But with Henny's on-base duties, and Mix's occasional leaves, they had far more time together than ever before in Sweden.

Henny and Mix in Sweden.
(Photograph from The History of a Resistance Group.)

*Two faces of Henny, above in a Danish Brigade
uniform in Sweden, below on the pistol range.
(Photographs from Henny's Historie.)*

Henny and Mix were both safe and close together, for the moment at least, and their relationship continued to deepen. But the rest of 1944 was frustrating for both of them, especially for Mix.

Their country was visible from the Swedish coast but beyond reach. Their ability to strike the Nazi war machine—so essential to both of them—was on hold. And, for so long as the war continued and Henny and Mix remained in exile, Henny refused to marry him. It was simply a question of waiting for the right time and place. For Henny, a period of exile in Sweden, separated from and unable to communicate with their families, was neither the right time nor place.

Gerda III: Resistance at Sea

The history of Holger Danske 2—one of hard-hitting attacks and dramatic escapes—demonstrates the need for vessels that could come to the aid of resistance fighters and their families. Henny wrote in 1980, and stated in her 1994 interview, that *Gerda III* did just that, saving "people [in] the resistance movement." For the months that Henny remained in Denmark after the October 1943 rescue—as a member of a resistance group that needed to smuggle people to and from Sweden—she undoubtedly played a role in getting "people from the resistance movement" onto *Gerda III* when the need arose, just as she had played a vital role in getting Jews onto the boat when they had to be evacuated. Until her own escape, there would often have been no reason for HD2, or for the resistance leaders at Staffeldt's bookstore, to look further than Henny and her boat.

Gerda III's crew also developed connections to other resistance groups that needed the same type of help. Indeed, transporting resistance fighters after October 1943 was a return to the kind of work they had performed before the Jewish rescue for Ejler and Ingolf Haubirk, and the Haubirk resistance group was still very much in operation after the Jewish rescue was completed. With the lighthouse in enemy hands, the dangers had increased substantially since the early missions for the Haubirks. *Gerda III* now had to carry resisters all the way to Sweden (or at least into Swedish waters) rather than to the lighthouse. The longer distance and more intense scrutiny by the German navy made the chances of detection even greater, and German patrol boats were increasingly likely to shoot at any vessel suspected of aiding the resistance. But *Gerda III*'s crew never quit.

In the aftermath of the Jewish rescue, during the final eighteen months of war, *Gerda III* also became an escape route for Allied bomber crews and other airmen whose planes had been too heavily damaged in the skies over Germany and other Nazi territory to return to their bases in England. Airmen who made emergency landings in Denmark or parachuted onto Danish soil were sheltered in Danish homes, hospitals, and other locations until they could be taken by Holger Danske or other resistance groups to one of the few boats—*Gerda III* among them—that dared cross Nazi-controlled waters with Allied fliers and other combatants hidden in their holds. It was another phase in which Mogens Staffeldt and Christian Kisling were also active, and likely to have led persons pursued by the Nazis to *Gerda III*.

Kisling related in his recording that one of his first assignments as a member of Holger Danske was to extricate an Allied pilot who had been shot down over Denmark and was being held in a hospital, under German guard, with two broken legs. While a helpful nurse distracted the guards, Kisling and an assistant passed the pilot through a hospital window to Kisling's waiting ambulance. Kisling drove the flier to Copenhagen, dressed him in civilian clothes, and sent him to Sweden the next day. This, in Kisling's words, "was not the only time I was [sent] out to rescue British or American airmen, we were very successful at it." With his ever-growing ties to Holger Danske, to Mogens Staffeldt, and to others closely associated with Henny's group, the "we" almost certainly included *Gerda III*.

In Henny's words, *Gerda III* carried Danish resisters, their families, and Allied airmen to safety "all the way until the war ended." Indicating a shift from daylight to nighttime crossings, she stated that *Gerda III* carried these combatants and their families "not every night [unlike its daily daytime missions during the Jewish rescue operation] but a couple of times a week."[137] "Thanks to *Gerda III* and her crew," Henny wrote, "about 1,000 people [300 Jews and 700 other Nazi targets] escaped falling into the Nazis' claws."

Henny's escape demonstrates the perils that *Gerda III*'s crew faced during their 1944 and 1945 rescue missions. Each time that *Gerda III* took resistance fighters and bomber crews across the Øresund, it faced the same type of enemy patrol boats that shot at Henny during her escape, and it did so without her police boat's ability to outrun the enemy. *Gerda III*'s crew had to rely more on cunning than speed.

THE DANGER THAT *GERDA III* FACED was also demonstrated by the fate of another rescuer, Erling Kiaer, who continued this line of work after the Jewish rescue operation was completed. Kiaer was a founder and leading member of a rescue group that its members deceptively named the Elsinore Sewing Club. The Sewing Club transported many hundreds of Jews to safety from points north of Copenhagen, and went on to save hundreds of other people targeted by the Nazis. It began by escorting Jews to hiding places in coastal towns near Elsinore (Helsingør in the Danish spelling), finding boat owners willing to transport them to Sweden, and then bringing the Jews to prearranged departure points. The system worked well during the first few days of the rescue, but Gestapo crackdowns in local ports from Snekkersten to Gilleleje—the range of the Sewing Club's operation—made it increasingly difficult to recruit enough boats and to get the refugees safely on board them. A different approach was needed, and Kiaer had the answer.

Swept along by Kiaer's confidence, and by their determination to see this through, the four leaders of the Elsinore Sewing Club decided to acquire and operate their own boat. Their brief experience convinced them that the best approach was to cross their portion of the Øresund at night, using a small vessel that refugees could board a short distance off a beach rather than in a tightly enclosed harbor. The fact that none of the group's members had ever operated a boat did not deter them. Kiaer, a bookbinder by trade, was confident that intuition and a little practice would enable him to navigate an unlit boat through the night, rendezvous with Jews who were waiting out of sight on the edges of a dark beach, and pick his way past German patrol boats to harbors on the other side of the Øresund. He became their captain and, surprisingly, he turned out to be right.

Their first boat proved the concept but was inadequate and quickly replaced. The second boat, known as the "*02*" boat, was faster and was used with great success. Kiaer piloted this twenty-one-foot wooden boat (now on display in the United States Holocaust Memorial Museum in Washington, DC) on many well-planned escape missions. Capitalizing on the short distance that separated Elsinore and the surrounding coast from Sweden, Kiaer completed an amazing three and sometimes four passages per night at the height of the Jewish rescue operation.

By the end of October, the nature of Kiaer's missions began to change, and so did the forces arrayed against him and other Danes who defied the Nazis at sea. Paralleling the changes in *Gerda III*'s missions, Kiaer was crossing with fewer Jews on board (the great majority having already been brought to safety) and with an ever-increasing number of combatants—saboteurs, other Danish freedom fighters, and Allied airmen—occupying the space in Kiaer's cabin that Jewish refugees once occupied. The Nazis' reaction to this new phase, and to the embarrassment caused by the success of the Jewish rescue fleet, was plain to see. By November, the Germans were deploying faster, more maneuverable, and more heavily armed patrol boats, each with a Gestapo agent on board.

Kiaer's response was to get a faster boat.

The Elsinore Sewing Club's third boat, dubbed the "*03*," was in operation by the beginning of 1944 and was soon put to the test. On the night of January 20, 1944, Kiaer piloted the boat to a beach north of Elsinore to pick up seven people—a group that included several Jews who had remained behind to fight in the resistance and two other saboteurs. They were brought to the meeting place by two other core members of the Sewing Club: a police detective named Thormod Larsen and a police department clerk named Ove Bruhn. Bruhn helped each refugee cross the distance from the beach to the boat. Suddenly, just as the last refugee was lifted aboard, shouting was heard on the beach, followed first by a gunshot and then by a continuous volley of gunfire. Kiaer quickly pulled Ove Bruhn on board and sped out of range—not entirely unscathed. One refugee was hit by three bullets, sustaining wounds from which he later recovered in Sweden. Four other bullets went through the hull, and twelve lodged in the hull planks. Back on the beach, Larsen—felled by the first shots and too far from the boat to be helped by Kiaer—lay critically injured with four bullet wounds. The Nazis took Larsen to an Elsinore hospital, evidently intent on keeping him alive long enough to interrogate him. Despite the twenty-four-hour guard that the Nazis stationed outside his room, other members of the Sewing Club managed to smuggle Larsen's near lifeless body out of the hospital and into Kisling's ambulance. Kisling then sped Larsen to Bispebjerg Hospital, where he was given emergency surgery and then whisked away for more treatment at a secret location. A year passed before he was well enough to be removed to Sweden.[138]

The incident forced a suspension of the Sewing Club's activities. Rightfully convinced that an informer had revealed the Club's leadership to the Gestapo, Kiaer went underground with his family until his wife and two children were evacuated to Sweden on February 20, 1944—the same day that Henny was taken to the coast for her evacuation. Kiaer then returned to the water, continuing his dangerous crossings for three more months.

On the night of May 12, 1944—after completing 142 illegal crossings—Kiaer's luck ran out. Kiaer set out from Sweden at 9:30 p.m., as he had done many times before, to return to Denmark. As soon as he left Swedish waters, he was intercepted and surrounded by six German patrol boats. His attempt to reverse course and escape was cut short by a burst of machine gun fire that put his boat out of commission. Kiaer spent the rest of the war in Nazi prisons in Denmark and the infamous Porta Westphalica prison camp in Germany.

THE CREW OF GERDA III assumed these risks and more. Henny's father, Paul Sinding, later wrote that, after Henny led the Lighthouse and Buoy Service into "resistance work," he followed her lead. Under his supervision, the Service's role in the resistance was elevated from participation by individual crewmen and other employees to a policy of the Service itself. In 1944, the Service began to supply the resistance with explosives that it kept on hand to clear wrecks and other hazards to navigation. It also smuggled out military equipment that was stored at the Royal Dockyards. And, as Paul Sinding wrote, it "acquired illegal radio transmitters" that the resistance needed to communicate with the SOE and other colleagues outside of Denmark—transmitters that the Service almost certainly brought across the Øresund from Sweden. Although unconfirmed, it would be logical to infer that the Service, and *Gerda III* in particular, also brought back more lethal equipment.

At about the same time that Henny was forced to flee to Sweden, *Gerda III* crewman Gerhardt Steffensen was similarly compelled to escape with his family. Whether his departure was prompted by his closeness to Holger Danske 2—as the timing would suggest—or by his role in other resistance activities, is unknown. What is known is that he entered a new phase of resistance work, very likely involving *Gerda III*, after he arrived in Sweden.

Gerhardt Steffensen played a leading role in the Swedish side of an operation that smuggled American weapons to the Danish resistance.[139] His counterparts on the Danish coast were the Haubirk brothers, who had already come to rely on *Gerda III*. The weapons smuggling operation went into high gear in August 1944 and continued through at least October 22, 1944, when Ejler Haubirk was shot dead by the Gestapo. During the operation, Gerhardt and his brother Martin repeatedly loaded weapons onto their boat, the *Nilfisken*, and sailed it from Limhamn to a rendezvous point midway across the Øresund. There, they transferred the weapons to a Danish boat to complete the mission. No writings identify the boat that took the weapons the rest of the way to Denmark, but *Gerda III* would have been a logical and, by August 1944, a compelling choice. The route from Limhamn to the weapons' destination would have intersected, or at least come close to, the route that *Gerda III* took to and from the Drogden Lighthouse every day. In an operation where the ability to trust the next person meant everything, there was nobody on the Danish coast that Gerhardt Steffensen could trust more than his *Gerda III* crewmates—people with whom he had sailed and defied the Nazis since the start of the occupation. Moreover, just as the Steffensen's were gearing up in Sweden, the Nazis decimated the ranks of the Dragør mariners who had made covert crossings for the resistance, and who might have provided alternatives to *Gerda III*.

Disaster struck Dragør's seafaring community on July 24, 1944, when the Gestapo killed the leader of an organization that arranged evacuations from Dragør, and seized a treasure trove of incriminating information. Three days later, the Gestapo put that information to use, arresting sixteen Dragør fishermen with ties to the resistance. Other Dragør captains who sailed for the resistance, including another Steffensen brother, Hans, escaped to Sweden.[140] These events would have made *Gerda III* an obvious choice to meet the *Nilfisken* at sea and bring its clandestine cargo to Danish soil. And by the summer of 1944, when the Lighthouse and Buoy Service was already delivering explosives and "illegal radio transmitters" to the resistance, there was every reason for the weapons smugglers to believe that Paul Sinding would back the plan if he was asked, and not be greatly disturbed if one of his crews participated in the plan without asking.

1945: The End of the Struggle

As 1944 drew to a close, Henny had been looking forward to celebrating New Year's Eve "with Mix and the boys" at his training camp. That night, she wrote, "Mix was determined that we should get married," something that had been a "recurring discussion for the last couple of months." Henny wanted to marry Mix, but she was determined to wait until the war and their exile was over. But waiting was not his style. As Henny realized when she first met Mix, "everything he undertook had to go fast." So, Henny wrote, "when we took leave" on January 2, with peace and marriage still months away, "we were both very unhappy." The following day, she received a brief message from his camp: "Mix has left."[141]

As soon as Henny and Mix parted, he gathered his weapon and ammunition, went to the narrow north end of the Øresund, stole a rowboat, and rowed back to Denmark. He arrived just south of Elsinore, cut through barbed wire that the Germans had laid across the beaches, and made it ashore. From there, in the shadow of Kronborg Castle, he resumed his war.

Little more than one-week later, Henny absorbed another blow when Danish radio reported that her father had been arrested by the Gestapo. Henny soon learned that the report was erroneous but not far off the mark. At 4:00 a.m. on January 10, Gestapo agents kicked open the door of her family's home and stormed in. Her father, with good reason, assumed they had come for him. Had the Gestapo been aware of the smuggling activities that Paul Sinding later acknowledged, and of *Gerda III*'s ongoing role in the resistance— the known evacuations and the likely arms transports—he would have been arrested, interrogated, and very likely executed. He was therefore shocked to learn that the Gestapo had not come for him but for Henny's eighteen- year-old brother, Carsten. Carsten would not be heard from again until the end of the war.

Henny did not have to wait that long to hear from Mix. Danish vessels traveling between Denmark and Sweden operated an illegal courier service for the resistance. Availing himself of that, Mix wrote in a February 3, 1945, letter to Henny:

> My moods are great now…. There is plenty of work here for me but terrible conditions…. I am used to having co-workers. The ones I have now are not as good as my old friends…. Oh how I miss all of you….
> My dearest, we will meet again at the seashore.

On February 6, Mix wrote a letter that expressed grave concerns about his present position, coupled with his hopes for the future:

I do not feel very comfortable with any of my current co-workers. Otherwise my work is going pretty well.... Being here is a little like driving along a cliff. I have thought several times that my luck was running out, but was fortunate at the last minute to find a way out.... Here we are expecting the end [of the war] very soon and our optimism is great.

Mix's last letter, dated February 23, reached Henny on March 4.

My team had a terrible disappointment. A job did not succeed. It was a very good job but it did not go as planned.... [H]ad it succeeded it would have made the world news....

Otherwise things are going well but how I long for you. You would be such a help to me now, but we had our time and it will come again when this is over.

The job that "did not go as planned" would indeed have made the news. Mix planned to cut off coal shipments to Germany, and impede the Nazis' ability to take any large vessels in or out of Copenhagen, by blowing up a coal ship at the port entrance. Exactly where the job went wrong is unknown. What is known is that at 2:00 a.m. on February 27, a Danish informer—possibly one of the co-workers that Mix "did not feel very comfortable with"—led the Gestapo to Mix's apartment. Mix shot the informer and one of the Gestapo agents but was shot in the leg and captured. On March 3, the day before Henny received his last letter, Mix was killed during an attempt to escape from guards who were taking him to face a firing squad.[142] He was eighteen days short of his twenty-second birthday.

On May 4, 1945, two months after Mix was killed, the BBC announced that German forces in Denmark, Holland, and Norway surrendered. Henny heard the broadcast at the Danish Brigade camp in Sweden where she was stationed. The next day, her unit crossed the Øresund on the ferry *Holger Danske*, tracing the route that Mix had taken in January when he left Sweden and rowed back to Denmark to rejoin the war. Henny said in 1994 that she was sorry she did not have the same chance. In her words, "we arrived at Helsingør" to a "very great welcome," but it "was not the way we intended to come back to Denmark. We had intended to come back to fight."

Chapter Seven

HOMECOMING AND REMEMBRANCE

Henny and the Resistance

FOR NEARLY FORTY YEARS after the war, Henny and most other Holger Danske 2 survivors seldom wrote or spoke about their resistance activities to anyone beyond their immediate families and fellow resistance fighters. Henny told her 1994 interviewer "it was as if…we had to forget it and we never talked about it…. Everybody was so busy getting on in life you simply stopped talking about the war…. You would never ask a person what he did during the war… and you would never dream of telling what you were doing yourself. It was just taboo."

Henny, of course, could not simply "forget it." The best of it and the worst of it stayed with her. She relished her role in saving hundreds of lives but was haunted by one death—Mix's. For the rest of her life, she carried the burden of believing that Mix would have lived if she had agreed to marry him on his timetable rather than hers.

In all probability, that burden was undeserved. Just as Henny "intended to come back to fight," Mix clearly intended to do so. The man for whom everything "had to go fast" would wait only so long for the Danish Brigade to go into action. The navy cadet who tried to row to Sweden to rejoin Denmark's surviving warships for a sea battle that never materialized would have wanted to row back to strike another blow, regardless of Henny's decision, before the war ended. His letters to Henny made it clear that he loved her no less for her decision and that she remained a powerful reason to live.

Henny never completely let go of Mix. In more than one sense, he was never far away.

On the northern outskirts of Copenhagen, Mindelunden, the "Grove of Remembrance" has become the hallowed resting place for members of the Danish resistance who lost their lives during the war. It occupies the site of a Danish army base that the Nazis overran in August 1943 and turned into a killing field. Three bronze posts stand on a secluded lawn at one end of the Grove, each cast from a wooden post that stood on the same spot. Captured resistance fighters were tied to the posts and executed by Nazi firing squads. Mix was being taken there when he made his final escape attempt. In death, he completed the journey. His body and those of another 196 resistance fighters who were executed by firing squads, or killed in nearby actions, were found at the site in makeshift graves when the war ended.

A few months later, on August 29, 1945, Mix and other freedom fighters whose bodies were unearthed at Mindelunden were given a hero's funeral. Their caskets, each carried on an open truck, were driven through the streets of Copenhagen in a procession led by Denmark's King Christian X. Rows of their countrymen, standing shoulder to shoulder all along the route, showered the procession with flowers as bells pealed in every steeple. Mix and his comrades were laid to rest in dignified graves surrounding a monument that demonstrates the high esteem in which they are held. Another thirty-one graves of resistance fighters whose bodies were recovered from Porta Westphalica and other Nazi prisons, and 157 memorial plaques for resistance fighters who died at those prisons or simply disappeared without a trace, were added at a later date. In all, 379

Danish freedom fighters who perished at the hands of the Nazis are memorialized there. Henny was a regular visitor.

The process of "getting on in life" was harder and longer than Henny's comment about post-war life suggested. For two months after she returned to Denmark, Henny remained in the Danish Brigade, serving with a unit that was sent to clear land mines that the Nazis had planted in Jutland.

When Henny's unit was disbanded on July 10, 1945, she travelled to Holland, as part of a Danish Red Cross mission, to help save the lives of Dutch children who had been liberated from Nazi concentration camps. They were children, in Henny's words, who had emerged "completely emaciated" and alone.[143] Most had been freed from Bergen-Belsen where another young Dutch girl, Ann Frank, died of typhus and malnutrition a few weeks before Allied troops reached the camp's gates.

Travelling in Red Cross truck convoys, Henny escorted the children from Holland to Denmark, where they were nursed back to health over a period of months, and then brought them back home to the Netherlands. Her travels to and from Holland with the young concentration camp survivors left an indelible impression on her of the horrors from which she and the crew of *Gerda III* had spared so many others. And it left a profound impression of the price that Nazi Germany paid for its atrocities. The convoy's route between Denmark and Holland passed through what Henny described as "the heap of rubble" that was once Hamburg—a city that waves of British and American bombers leveled, with more than 4,600 tons of explosives, in July 1943.

After Henny and her colleagues returned the Dutch children to health, and to their homeland, Henny went to Norway "because there were also many in [that country] who had starved" during the war.[144]

And so, for the better part of a year after the Nazis surrendered, Henny helped others recover from their trauma while she sought to get her own bearings in a world without the great love and the great purpose that had propelled her since 1943. Only then was she able to put the war behind her and "get on in life."

By 1946, she began to see the Øresund, once again, as she had before the war. She returned to the Dragon sloop that she raced before the Jewish rescue operation caused her to put such things aside. A newspaper photograph taken that year as Henny prepared her boat for a race captured some of the attributes—her beauty, her athleticism, her sense of purpose—that no doubt had caught Mix's eye. It captures a quality that would have given heart to a refugee whose life was in her hands, and confidence to a resistance leader assembling a team for a perilous mission.

Henny, raising sail at Hellerup in 1946.
(Photograph courtesy of the Sundø family.)

Nearly two years after the war ended, in March 1947, Henny married another member of the armed resistance, Erling Sundø. Erling was part of Henny's past as well as her future. Before the war, he pursued Henny romantically, and in his racing sloop, at the Hellerup Sailing Club where Henny competed against Erling and other boys. Henny tended to remain boat lengths ahead of her sailing competitors and her suitors. For Erling, who fell into both categories, it had been a frustrating period.

The war gave Henny and Erling more in common—the resistance, their flight to Sweden, and their time in the Danish Brigade. Erling and his brother Erik had joined the uprising that followed the Nazis' attempt to capture and deport Denmark's Jews. They specialized in stealing weapons from the Nazis for a resistance group known as the Homefront. Erik's luck ran out in May 1944, when the Gestapo captured him and sent him off to Porta Westphalica—a place that he barely survived and that he bore the scars of for the rest of his life. Erling, with the Gestapo on his heels, was evacuated to Sweden after Erik's arrest.

Erling spent time in Sweden with Henny and Mix, and he understood their relationship. Henny, Erling, and Erik each lived with their ghosts and understood each other as only people who shared such a past could do.

On July 16, 1947, four months after Henny and Erling were married, the last of the Danish freedom fighters who had perished at the hands of the Nazis were buried and accounted for. It was a day of reunion and remembrance. Henny and other survivors of HD2, including Jørgen Kieler, his brother Flemming, and his two sisters—all of whom miraculously survived Nazi prisons—were at Mindelunden that day. So, too, was Mogens Staffeldt, who the Nazis had mistakenly released and who escaped to Sweden while the Nazis sought to recapture him. The head of the Danish underground in Sweden welcomed Staffeldt and promptly put him in charge of transporting resistance fighters and supplies across the Øresund.[145]

Klaus Rønholdt, whom Jørgen Kieler had carried through the snow at Jutland, and Jørgen Staffeldt, whom the Gestapo had captured when they lured him out of a meeting with Henny and Mix, were among those who perished in Nazi captivity in Germany. They were remembered at Mindelunden along with Mix, John, and other members of Holger Danske, whom the Nazis killed on Danish soil.

It became Jørgen Kieler's task, as he put it, "to give a last salute to the dead."[146] Kieler spoke of his time at Porta Westphalica, drawing inspiration from the final hours that he spent with his fellow prisoner Jørgen Staffeldt. As Staffeldt's body broke down under the strain of forced labor and malnutrition, Kieler—who was not much better off at the time—cared for him in whatever small ways one prisoner could aid another. Kieler was with Staffeldt when he died on Christmas Day, 1944.[147] Staffeldt, Kieler said, embodied the spirit of the resistance fighters at Porta Westphalica and elsewhere. In Kieler's words:

> In the midst of this small but utterly evil world where human beings were slowly being reduced to hunted animals, he emanated a strange restfulness, which was marked by both humility and pride.... [A] slight but victorious smile crossed his lips. They had tried to remove his right to be a human being, to love humanity, and they had lost.[148]

Henny's effort to "get on in life" in the post-war, post-Mix world was a journey in which her combination of humility, pride, and love of humanity was also evident. Without casting aside their memories of a lost love and lost comrades, Henny and Erling "got on," raised two daughters, and lived good lives.

Henny's daughters and nephews grew up in the homes of heroes and inherited a hero's perspective on the war and the resistance. Henny related the good and the bad and let her family know how she added it all up. She told them that the months she and her fellow resisters devoted to rescuing Denmark's Jews and waging war against the Nazis—months when they risked their lives and when friends and loved ones lost their lives—were months in which they felt more alive than ever before. The voids left by the loss of loved ones were easier to bear than the emptiness they would have felt if they had done nothing. Taking action against the evil in their midst, rather than tolerating it, enabled them to face the rest of their lives with satisfaction rather than shame. It was the right thing to do. It was the only thing to do.

Despite her burdens, Henny went through life very much the person she had been before she put her life on the line. For years after the war, she continued to race sailboats on the Øresund, not far from where *Gerda III* made its dangerous wartime crossings, and she continued to win. In her later years, in her home in the seaside village of Charlottenlund, Henny continued to surround herself with her father's maritime paintings. One of them, a life-long favorite, depicts a *Gerda III* crewman climbing a buoy to service its light while two other crewmen stood by in a dinghy. It was a painting that had hung over her bed as a girl, and that she was once horrified to learn that her father had given to a friend who also admired it. After the war, the painting came back to her from that friend, with a thank you note for rescuing him on *Gerda III*. She hadn't recognized her father's friend when she took him to the Christianshavn warehouse or when she gave him a final push toward *Gerda III*'s cargo hold, but he had recognized her.

When Henny died on August 22, 2008, at age 87, she was remembered as a person who had been full of life. Hundreds of others remember her as a person who willingly risked her life to save theirs.

The Danish Jews

Nearly all of the Danish Jews who were forced to flee to Sweden returned to Denmark at the end of the war. Remarkably, most of those whom the Nazis deported to the Theresienstadt concentration camp also survived and returned to Denmark—thanks to the ongoing attention paid by people in Sweden and Denmark. There was also a small but significant third group of survivors: Jewish children who remained in Denmark throughout the war, safeguarded and nurtured in Danish homes.

Jews who escaped Denmark by boat were welcomed in Sweden—once the Swedish government overcame its reluctance to accept refugees—and welcomed again when they returned home. Swedes worked hand-in-hand with Danish groups to assist Denmark's Jews during their exile. Leo Goldberger, the cantor's son who had fled with his family from Dragør, wrote in *The Rescue of the Danish Jews* that Sweden's October 2, 1943, broadcast, extending a welcome to all Danish Jews who could reach its shores, "spelled the beginning of that country's magnificent humanitarian contributions, which exceeded all expectations, and for which it can be justly proud." One joint endeavor was the creation of a school system for Jewish refugees and the children of resistance fighters who were forced to flee Denmark. Buildings supplied by Swedes, textbooks smuggled from Denmark, and a faculty composed of refugee teachers and university professors, enabled young Goldberger, Aaron Engelhardt, and hundreds of other school-age refugees to make the most of their time in Sweden while preparing for their return to Denmark.

When the Danish Jews came home at war's end, they generally found their property as they had left it. Aaron Engelhardt, who reached Sweden with his family on *Gerda III* in early October 1943, wrote that his family's apartment had been kept in a state of readiness for their return, and had been "cleaned and tidied up" by Christian friends when their return was imminent. Leo Goldberger had the same experience. Like Aaron, Leo and his family returned to an apartment and belongings that, in his words, "had been left undisturbed, ready for us to resume our lives among our many Danish friends." His father resumed his role as the cantor of the Great Synagogue, leading the reconstituted congregation in prayer. Their experience was indicative of what most of the Danish Jews found upon their return. With few exceptions, Danish law had kept their property intact, neighbors had tended their homes, and associates had preserved their businesses.[149]

Gert Lilienfeldt, whose parents had saved him from Nazi Germany by sending him to Denmark when he was fourteen years old, and whom Henny and the crew of *Gerda III* saved from the Nazis when he was nineteen years old, decided to go no further than Denmark when he returned from Sweden. In Germany, there was nothing to return to. He confirmed that his parents, with whom he lost contact in 1941, had perished. The rest of his family, whose German roots went back four centuries, had all but vanished, consumed by the Holocaust. In the midst of the horror Danes had befriended him, made him a part of their family, saved him, and embraced him again when the war ended. Remaining in Denmark until his death in 2006, he married, raised three children, and established a successful business.

THE HIGH PERCENTAGE OF DANISH JEWS who survived the ordeal of captivity in the Theresienstadt Concentration Camp was a victory of another sort, and proof that the effort to save Denmark's Jews did not end with their capture. Theresienstadt was not a death camp, in the sense that it did not have gas chambers. But it was a place where many people died of starvation, disease, and exhaustion, and it was a way station on the road to the death camps. Of the roughly 140,000 Jews who the Nazis transported to Theresienstadt, 33,000 died in that camp and another 90,000 were sent onward to die in Nazi gas chambers—a *mortality* rate of nearly ninety percent. Yet, of the nearly five hundred Danish Jews who were sent to Theresienstadt, all but fifty-one survived—a *survival* rate of nearly ninety percent.

The extraordinary survival rate of the Danish Jews resulted from persistent intervention by still functioning remnants of the Danish government and by the Swedish government. After months of wrangling, the Danish Red Cross was given permission to inspect the camp on June 23, 1945, two and one-half weeks after the Normandy invasion. The Nazis used the weeks before the visit to create the illusion of a humane environment—alleviating overcrowding by transporting three thousand prisoners to die at Auschwitz before the inspectors arrived.[150]

When the inspectors departed, most of the props that the Nazis carted out for the day, including decent meals, disappeared. But continuing pressure led to some longer lasting improvements for the Danish Jews, including deliveries of food packages from Denmark and Sweden that cut the mortality rate of the Danish prisoners in half.[151]

In February 1945, two weeks after Soviet forces reached the gates of Auschwitz, Danes and Swedes stepped up pressure on Nazi Germany to release the Jews and other prisoners who had been captured in Scandinavia. The negotiations, led by the Denmark's Nils Svenningsen (the senior remaining official at the Ministry of Foreign Affairs) and by Sweden's Count Folke Bernadotte (the nephew of Sweden's king and vice president of the Swedish Red Cross), were a painstaking process that began by securing incremental improvements in the lives of some prisoners—including the ability to get medicine and food to captured resisters—and led to more sweeping breakthroughs in early April. The result was a series of convoys, known ever since as the "White Buses," that were sent from Sweden to retrieve Nazi-held prisoners and bring them to freedom. As the initial goal—the repatriation of Scandinavian prisoners—was achieved, the mission was broadened to rescue thousands of additional concentration camp prisoners.

The first group of White Buses arrived on April 9, 1945 at Porta Westphalica and other parts of the Neuengamme Concentration Camp complex, where many Danish resisters had already perished and where others clung to life by a thread. Kieler wrote that "this help came early enough to save four of the HD2 saboteurs who had escaped execution and been deported to Germany" but "too late to save the young student Klaus Ronholdt...."[152]

Six days later, additional efforts to obtain the release of the Danish Jews paid off. On April 15, 1945, 425 Jewish prisoners stepped through the gates of Theresienstadt onto a fleet of twenty-three white buses—a Red Cross and Swedish flag painted on each side to deter attacks by the forces still battling on land and in the skies over Germany—and began the trip to Sweden.[153] They were the first Theresienstadt prisoners to leave for a destination other than the death camps.

For two days the buses travelled through Germany—through the ruins of fire-bombed Dresden, through Potsdam neighborhoods that were still smoldering from the prior night's air raid, through an utterly destroyed landscape—as Allied bombs continued to fall around them. It was, in effect, the first bus tour of the fallen Reich. In a reversal of what had been the wartime order, Denmark's Jews could look upon the ashes of Hitler's Germany from a place of relative safety. When the White Buses crossed the Danish border, the people of the frontier town Padborg greeted the passengers with sandwiches, flowers, and invitations to their homes. Then, following the terms of the agreement under which they were released, the buses and their passengers continued through Copenhagen to ferries that took them across the Øresund to Sweden—one year and seven months after their relatives and friends made the crossing.[154] There, they had to await the end of the war, only a few weeks later, before they could go home.

FOR SOME, RETURNING TO DENMARK from nineteen months as concentration camp prisoners or as refugees in Sweden meant being reunited with children they left behind. Research conducted by the Danish Jewish Museum established that at least 139 children from Danish Jewish families—a number described as an "absolute minimum" and likely understatement—remained with Christian families after their parents escaped to Sweden or were captured by the Nazis. These so called "hidden children" ranged at the start of the rescue from only a few days old to seventeen. Sixty percent were less than five years old.[155]

For those parents who chose to leave children in the care of Christian relatives and friends rather than attempt to escape with them, the gut-wrenching decision reflected the parents' profound fear of what might befall their families while trying to reach a rescue boat or during the crossing itself. Without question, they felt that entrusting their children to Christian families in Denmark would maximize their children's chances of survival.

As the war dragged on, and parents who managed to escape found security in Sweden, arrangements were made through resistance channels to reunite about one third of the hidden children with their parents—usually transporting them, between two and nine months after the October rescue operation, on vessels such as *Gerda III*. Ironically, these belated crossings significantly increased the dangers that the children faced. Vessels making illegal crossings after October 1943 were far more likely to be carrying combatants and weapons along with any remaining refugees, and—as participants in the new era of open warfare between the Nazis and the Danish resistance—were far more likely to be fired upon by Nazi forces.

The remaining two thirds of the hidden children remained in Denmark, for the rest of the war, with the families that had taken them in. Most of these children were hidden in plain sight. They were integrated into their foster families and treated as one more daughter or son. Keeping them safe was a community endeavor, as the sudden appearance of another child at school or elsewhere would hardly go unnoticed. Active assistance from merchants, farmers, and others was needed to procure food and other essentials for which rationing stamps—doled out in precise amounts for each parent and child—had to be presented. A helpful church official or public servant could invariably be found to provide fictitious baptism and birth certificates. And everyone had to be alert, ready to pull a child indoors, send them down to a cellar, or quickly shift them to another location, when Gestapo forces came too close to home. It was a complicated matter, requiring broad support, yet not one of Denmark's hidden children was ever discovered by the Nazis.

TODAY, SONS AND DAUGHTERS of Denmark's World War II Jewish population, as well as some of those who rode the rescue craft as children, live on in Denmark. Copenhagen's Great Synagogue, where Rabbi Melchior told his congregants that they had to leave and go into hiding, also lives on—not as a relic of a bygone people but as a vibrant meeting place for Denmark's Jewish community. The torahs, which had been sent for safekeeping in nearby Trinitatis Church at the start of the rescue, are back in the Synagogue's ark, and in use. During this author's visit on a sunny June day in 2014, a day like many others, the synagogue was filled with Jews and fellow Danes celebrating a wedding. At the entrance to the synagogue, a young member of the congregation stood vigil. A new surge of anti-Semitism in some quarters of Europe, and in some immigrant communities within Denmark, made it prudent to be on guard. Eight months later another congregant, standing guard on the same spot, was murdered by the son of Palestinian immigrants. Two Danish policemen were wounded as they defended the synagogue during the same attack. But on the night of the wedding, the young man standing watch was unafraid. Well versed in the lessons of the past, and well aware of the perils of today, he remained confident about the future—confident that his countrymen will continue to embrace the centuries-old traditions that sparked the Danish resistance and dealt Nazi persecution its most striking defeat.

Chapter Eight

REFLECTIONS ON THE RESCUE

IN 1968, ISRAEL AND DENMARK held simultaneous ceremonies to mark the twenty-fifth anniversary of the Danish rescue. In Israel, a sculpture of a Danish fishing boat and a plaque describing the events of October 1943 were unveiled at the newly renamed "Denmark Square" in Jerusalem. The plaque concluded, fittingly:

> Danish courage and Swedish generosity gave indelible proof of human values in a time of barbarism. Israel and Jews all over the world will never forget.

Henny, *Gerda III*'s crew, and other Danes on the front lines of the rescue effort, clearly exhibited remarkable courage. Henny and *Gerda III*'s crew had to have known of the catastrophes that were befalling rescuers and refugees along the Zealand coast—the gunfire directed at the *Dannebrog* as it sought to leave Gilleleje's harbor; the arrest of the fishermen at Snekkersten; the arrests of scores of refugees at Gilleleje, Dragør, and other harbors; the shooting death of Claus Heillesen at Taarbæk; and the destruction of the boat that hit a mine off Dragør. That none of this deterred them is a testament to their courage.

The overwhelming success of the rescue operation has led some to suggest that Nazi forces in Denmark lacked the ruthlessness that the Nazis demonstrated in other countries—even after the months of August to October 1943 in which the Nazis declared martial law, sent in the Gestapo to hunt down and execute resisters, and attempted to capture and send all of Denmark's Jews to the concentration camps. It has also been suggested that German battlefield losses, mainly on the Eastern Front, made Nazi forces in October 1943 more reluctant to commit war crimes for which they might soon be held accountable. Neither theory holds up.

The manner in which the Gestapo pursued, and in some cases tortured and executed members of Holger Danske and other resistance groups, demonstrates that the Gestapo wielded as much power in Denmark after martial law was imposed as they did in other occupied countries, and that they used it ruthlessly. Any notion that battlefield losses caused the Nazis to shrink from further atrocities is also belied by their relentless efforts to exterminate Europe's Jews everywhere outside of Denmark. Events in Hungary are particularly telling. Germany occupied Hungary in March 1944 after Hitler lost faith in the reliability of Hungary's fascist government. Even though the Nazis occupied Hungary five months *after* the Danes thwarted the Nazi plan to deport Denmark's Jews, the Nazis managed to deport 440,000 Hungarian Jews, mainly to Auschwitz, in a mere two months. They killed more than half a million Hungarian Jews before the end of the war.[156]

No external factors can account for the success of the Danish rescue. Chronologically, it took place when the defeat of Nazi Germany was more distant than it was when the Nazis slaughtered the Hungarian Jews. Geographically, no country was closer to the heart of the beast or had fewer natural defenses than Denmark. The difference could only have come from within.

In at least three respects, it clearly did so.

First, the spontaneous national movement to rescue the Jews caught the Gestapo by surprise and produced too many escape routes in too little time for the Gestapo to seal them off. For every informer who tipped the Gestapo to hiding places and escape routes, there were hundreds of rescuers who created new hiding places and new pathways to freedom. As Holocaust scholar Leni Yahil put it, even though the Danish people and their leaders had demonstrated solidarity with the Jews from the beginning of the occupation, and made it plain that they did not regard Jews as a people apart but as fellow countrymen,

> the rescue operation nevertheless came as a surprise—no one could have foreseen that in the hour of need the mass of the nation would give this identification the full force of action. No other example had ever been known.[157]

Second, the resistance movement, which responded to the attempted deportation of the Jews by launching new waves of attacks on military production facilities and German installations throughout Denmark, diverted the Gestapo from pursuing Jews to defending the German supply chain.

Third, the moral example set by the Danes appears to have had some impact on the forces arrayed against the Jews—not on the Gestapo and other Nazi zealots but, at a very minimum, on the occasional patrol boat officer or sentry whose moral impulses had not been wholly extinguished and could yet be revived. The Danes' clear commitment to protecting the lives of their Jewish countrymen made it plain to Duckwitz and others that any risks they took to save Jewish lives would not be in vain—that the Danes would fully utilize whatever opportunity was given to them to save the lives of their Jewish countrymen. Without that certainty, Duckwitz would have been less likely to jeopardize his own life by revealing—and hence subverting—his government's plan to annihilate Denmark's Jews.

These three things are true, and they present one level of explanation. But there is something deeper—something that explains why these things came to be true. For generations, while other cultures kept anti-Semitism and other ancient hatreds simmering beneath the surface, ready to be fanned into a conflagration, Danes followed a different course. That course is evidenced by seventeenth century royal decrees welcoming Jews to Denmark; eighteenth century decrees granting Jews full access to craft guilds and learned professions; nineteenth century decrees guaranteeing Jews full citizenship and equality under the law; and a twentieth century statute—enacted in February 1939 as a barrier against the spread of Nazi anti-Semitism—that made it a crime to "incite hatred against any section of the Danish population by reason of religion, origin or citizenship."[158] The law was Denmark's response to Krystallnacht, when Nazi mobs attacked synagogues and Jewish-owned homes and businesses throughout Germany and Austria. The argument presented in Parliament in support of the bill, as reported by Danish journalist and historian Bo Lindegaard in *A Short History of Denmark in the 20th Century,* was that

> anti-Semitism was not only an insult to the Jews, but as much a threat against the very foundation of the democracy framing Danish society. Once the notion of second-rate citizens was adopted, the illness would spread and poison society as a whole.

The argument grasped what had already happened in Nazi Germany, and foretold what was yet to befall Nazi Germany in the years ahead. It recognized the historical truth that movements built upon hate are invariably consumed by it in the end.

This view was embraced by Denmark's leading religious as well as secular institutions. Yale history professor Jaroslav Pelikan, whose field was the history of Christianity, opined that "the events of October 1943"—the immediate, widespread, and courageous outpouring of support for Denmark's Jews—were "the moral fruits" of work done a century earlier by a person Pelikan described as "the greatest spiritual force in Denmark's history." The legacy of Nikolai F. S. Grundtvig, of whom Pelikan spoke, was a theology summed up by the motto: "First a human being, then a Christian, this alone is life's order." The "immediate and ineluctable corollary," as Pelikan put it, is that people "are bound to one another with ties more profound than any of the barriers that human history, including the history of religion, may have constructed."[159] When Hal Koch, in September 1942, launched the series of speeches that rallied Danes to actively defend their democratic values and tradition of religious freedom, he made Grundtvig's teachings a central theme of his talks. When the bishops of the Danish Lutheran Church wrote their October 3, 1943 letter, calling upon all church members to "fight to preserve the freedom of our Jewish brothers and sisters," they were following the path that Grundtvig had charted for the Church in the 1800s.

Denmark's secular and religious institutions combined to build a consensus in support of democracy and religious freedom that withstood Nazi propaganda. Although Danes were exposed to competing messages throughout the five-year occupation—including a barrage of Nazi radio broadcasts and publications—they were unswayed by appeals to jettison the values that had sustained them and enriched their lives. In words that highlight the enduring relevance of Denmark's World War II experience, Professor Steven Borish, another scholar and close observer of Danish culture wrote:

> The rescue of the Danish Jews took place because the Danish people knew who they were. All the Nazi propaganda had not been able to take that away from them, had not been able to instill in them the hopelessness, depersonalization and fragmentation, the schizoid sense of alienation and isolation from humanity, that the Nazis had been able to instill in the great majority of people whose lands they occupied during those years. The Nazis failed in their mission in Denmark. The Danish people had kept their democratic traditions alive, and the Jews became a living symbol of that tradition."[160]

Despite the bold actions that the Danes took to protect the rights and lives of the Jews, some accounts of the rescue suggest that it fell short of Danish ideals in one respect: the need to pay passage fees to a portion of the fishermen who transported refugees to Sweden. To many Danes today, these charges are a stain on an otherwise shining effort. The self-criticism is largely undeserved.

The thousands of Danes who assisted the Jews on shore—those who provided warning and shelter, organized escape routes, and diverted Nazi forces with a surge of sabotage attacks on factories and transportation facilities—assumed the risks of imprisonment or death without any compensation at all. So, too, did mariners, such as the crew of *Gerda III*, who were in a position to help without being compensated. As for fishermen who did seek passage fees, most saw the payments as fair compensation for interrupting their livelihoods and assuming the risk that the Nazis would seize their boats and imprison or shoot them—fates that befell some fishermen and dockside helpers during the rescue effort.

The paramount factor in the analysis is that nobody was left behind for lack of funds. Danes from every walk of life saw to that.

Rescue groups found donations easy to come by and made payments on behalf of Jews and other refugees who could not afford to pay for their passage. As Jørgen Kieler related, it took two members of his group just twenty-four hours to raise a million Kroner "fortune" to help the Jews—enough to meet all of the group's rescue needs with money to spare for its armed resistance work. Similar donations flowed to doctors who ran the rescue operation at Bispebjerg Hospital. Ambulance driver and resistance leader Christian Kisling, who brought escaping Jews and other Nazi targets from the hospital to rescue boats, reported that money poured in to the hospital to aid its rescue efforts, and was readily available for the rescuers to use as needed. He related in his 1971 recording that "a cigar box [at the hospital] was our cash register [and] over one million kroner passed through" it. Other rescue groups similarly raised and doled out money, commensurate with the scale of their operations, to assure the uninterrupted evacuation of refugees within their care. Money came from Jews and non-Jews alike.

Refugees who acted independently of these groups, striking out on their own to secure passage, also found a helping hand. Leo Goldberger reported that a Lutheran minister provided his father, the

Cantor of Copenhagen's Great Synagogue, with the funds needed to secure passage for the five members of the Goldberger family. Leo wrote that the minister provided the funds "ostensibly as a loan" but "refused repayment after the war."[161] Presenting it as a loan simply conveyed confidence that the family would survive and return to Denmark when the Nazis were defeated. Many other individuals received similar "loans" or gifts, often through intermediaries from anonymous donors.

Doing their part to defend and save their Jewish countrymen came naturally to the Danes. Throughout Nazi occupied Europe, the answer to why so little effort was made to stop the murder of millions of Jews was often "what could we have done?" In Denmark, the answer to why so many rose up to save the Jews was often "what *else* could we have done?" Bo Lindegaard provided a more complete answer in another of his books, *Countrymen*. Drawing upon Danish history, Lindegaard wrote that because "anti-Semitism had not been allowed to take root" in Denmark, the "countless" Danes who sprang up to save the Jews regarded them simply as "distressed countrymen . . . who through no fault of their own were suddenly hit by a crime [perpetrated] by the occupying power." Danes therefore perceived both a "national duty" and a "personal responsibility" to come to the aid of the Jews—their fellow countrymen—"without regard to personal consequences."[162]

Henny embraced, and put into action, the personal and national duty of which Lindegaard wrote. Her statements that "we never divided [ourselves] up into Danes or Jews," that the Jews "were just Danes…like we were," and that the Nazi attack on the Jews was therefore an attack on "our Danish people," demonstrate the validity of Lidegaard's analysis. Through her words and deeds, Henny epitomized the ideals that made Denmark unique in Nazi-occupied Europe, and a shining example for the entire world.

Postscript

THE FINAL RESCUE

A GENERATION AFTER *GERDA III*'S wartime missions, much of the world had been turned upside down. For forty-five years after the Nazi surrender, Germany was split in two, the legacy of its post-war division between the Soviet Union and the Western Allies. In East Germany, struggling under Soviet domination, the former World War II oppressors had become the oppressed. On the other side of the partition, West Germany became a bastion of democracy on the front lines of the free world.

For East Germans, the Baltic Sea offered a slim chance of escape. The Baltic coastline runs in a continuous arc from East Germany to West Germany to Denmark. But the Iron Curtain descended on the sea as well as the land, and a line of East German watch towers and patrol boats made it all but impossible for residents of East Germany to reach the West German shore. The shortest distance from East Germany to Denmark was twenty-five miles, and the direct route ran through many of the same barriers that prevented escape to West Germany. But ten and one-half miles off the East German coast, a floating bit of Danish sovereignty, the lightship *Gedser Rev*, stood post in the Baltic. Through more than a decade of escape attempts, until the lightship was retired in 1972, its beacon guided both Øresund-bound ships and intrepid East German escapees who swam, paddled, or rowed toward its light. One escapee reached it in a homemade one-man submarine. Those who were strong and lucky enough to reach the *Gedser Rev*, a fraction of those who tried, were taken on board, cared for, and then whisked away to Denmark.

The engineer on the *Gedser Rev* during this period, Neils Gärtig, stated that "August to October was always the busiest period for us; the water would still be warm and the nights would still be long." East Germans who made it to the lightship during those long Baltic nights were given dry clothes and kept below deck, Gärtig explained, to keep them out of sight of the East German patrol boats and aircraft that kept a close watch on the lightship. Once the escapees were safely tucked away, the lightship would send a coded radio message—"we have run out of water"—to its headquarters. When the signal was received, *Gerda III* was dispatched to the lightship to take the escaping East Germans on board and carry them to freedom in Denmark.[163]

And so *Gerda III*, the boat that had earned its place in history by saving Jews and other people from the Nazis, ended its rescue career by saving German asylum seekers from Soviet tyranny. The one constant is that *Gerda III* was the instrument of people who perceived the right thing to do—and did it.

Research Notes and Acknowledgements

THE NATURE OF THE DANISH RESISTANCE movement, and the character of the people in the movement, left many of their individual efforts unrecorded. During the resistance movement, when any notes that fell into the wrong hands would have fatal consequences, nothing was written down. After the war, as Henny stated, "it was as if…we had to forget" and telling others what you did during the war "was just taboo." When their exploits were honored by others, the members of the Danish resistance declined individual recognition, preferring to emphasize the nationwide scope of the rescue effort and the armed resistance.

Yad Vashem, Israel's Holocaust memorial and archive, identifies and honors the "Righteous of the World" who risked their lives to save Jews. With respect to the Danes, Yad Vashem notes:

> The rescue operation by the Danish underground is exceptional because of the widespread agreement and resolve of many Danes from all walks of life—intellectuals, fishermen, priests, policemen, doctors, blue-collar workers—to save the Jews…. To pay tribute to this exceptional rescue operation and in the understanding that it was a joint effort, a tree was planted in the Avenue of the Righteous in honor of the Danish underground.

151

> Members of the Danish underground expressed their wish
> to Yad Vashem not to honor them as individuals....

In accordance with their wishes, a memorial plaque at the base of the tree reads simply, in English and Hebrew, "The Danish Resistance." Two other plaques, mounted elsewhere at Yad Vashem, honor "The People of Denmark" and King Christian X.

It is therefore difficult to tell the complete story of any individual's contribution to the rescue and the resistance movement, let alone the contributions of any individual boat. Fortunately, there is enough of a record to know much of what happened with respect to *Gerda III* and those associated with it.

Jørgen Kieler began to compile the history of Holger Danske 2, and of its members' role in the rescue, when he was freed from Nazi captivity in 1945. But he put the project aside for thirty-five years and did not return to it until 1980, when he contacted surviving members of the group and asked them to contribute to what he envisioned as a "collective" report. The result was a two-volume work, entitled *En Modstandsgruppes Historie (The History of a Resistance Group)*, that was privately published in 1982. Only three hundred copies were made for distribution to family members and a few select libraries. One set is available in the United States at the Harvard University library. Much of what appears in later books that have passages about *Gerda III* and Henny Sinding has been translated from this source. Kieler's volumes provide comprehensive first-hand accounts that are immeasurably valuable. Henny provided reports that Mix wrote during his ten months in Sweden, as well as her own narratives. Some of Henny's narratives also appear to have been written during her exile in Sweden, although parts were plainly updated or written after the war. My thanks go to Peter Bierrie and Kirsten Wendell, who volunteered to translate the sections used here. Additional translations, as well as help with my detective work, were enthusiastically provided by Rita Krone Kramer.

The United States Holocaust Memorial Museum in Washington, DC provided valuable videotaped interviews of Henny Sinding and

Jørgen Kieler. Henny's 1994 interview, *Oral History Interview with Henny Sundø* (her married name), is as close as one can come to having a conversation with Henny—and a unique opportunity to grasp her charm as well as her courage.

Members of the Sundø family generously gave their time, provided me with family photographs and other records, and enthusiastically supported my efforts to tell Henny's story. Together we strolled the streets where Henny lived; where she brought Jews on board *Gerda III*; where she hid with Mix (sleeping on the suitcases filled with grenades and guns after the Burmeister attack); and where *Gerda III* was stationed at the Royal Dockyards. They gave me a far more complete understanding of Henny's life than any writing could provide. And they gave me confidence that Henny and the Sundøs of her generation had passed the torch to the next generation.

Professor Leo Goldberger graciously gave his time to review a draft of this publication to assure that it accurately conveys the facts as well as the feelings of those who lived through the events, as he and his family did. He patiently responded to questions about his escape and the escapes of other refugees he knew during the exile and beyond. His information about the Elsinore Sewing Club and its rescue boats—including the vessel that he helped obtain for the United States Holocaust Memorial Museum—was a significant contribution to the description of the perils that the Danish resistance faced at sea. It has been an honor and a great benefit to have his input as a witness, a scholar, an interpreter, and a friend.

The Dragør Local Archive, a short walk from the dock where *Gerda III* was based for most of its working years, provided splendid photographs of *Gerda III* and its crew, as well as ship's documents and articles that provided valuable information about *Gerda III*'s role in the resistance and rescue operation. In Dragør's harbor, *Gerda IV*—a newer but still traditional wooden hull workboat—operates from the same dock that *Gerda III* used in peacetime, and heads out each day to do the same job. *Elisabeth K571*, a fishing boat that rescued more than seventy Danish Jews, and that has been meticulously restored by employees and volunteers of the Amager Museum, is tied up at the Dragør seawall when it is not retracing its escape route for the benefit of Danish students. The town's well-preserved lanes and cottages, an area of beauty and serenity today, make it easy to visualize the serious business of hide and seek that took place there in 1943. Special thanks go to Bente Walløe Poulsen (the director of the Dragør tourist office, a great-granddaughter of *Gerda III*'s first captain, and grandniece of its World War II crewmember Otto Andersen) for helping me navigate Dragør's treasure trove of information about *Gerda III* and for getting me on board *Gerda IV* for a trip to the Drogden Lighthouse.

Last, but certainly not least, my deep thanks go to my wife Lorraine who, throughout the project, was of the greatest assistance to my research and writing. Without her unwavering help and encouragement, this book would not exist.

Selected Bibliography

THERE ARE A NUMBER of noteworthy books and films about the rescue that I drew upon, in addition to Jørgen Kieler's two volume compilation, En *Modstandsgruppes Historie (The History of a Resistance Group)*. The best are noted below.

Flender, Harold, *Rescue in Denmark, How Occupied Denmark Rose as a Nation to Save the Danish Jews from Nazi Extermination*, Simon and Schuster, 1963.

Goldberger, Leo, *The Rescue of the Danish Jews: Moral Courage under Stress*, NYU Press, 1987.

Kieler, Jørgen, *Resistance Fighter: A Personal History of the Danish Resistance Movement*, 1940-1945, Gefen Publishing House, 2007.

Levine, Ellen, *Darkness over Denmark, the Danish Resistance and the Rescue of the Jews*, Holiday House, 2000.

Lidegaard, Bo, *Countrymen*, Alfred A. Knopf 2013.

Pundik, Herbert, *In Denmark it Could Not Happen: The Flight of the Jews to Sweden in 1943,* Gefen, 1998. (Note Chapter titled "Gerda III—The Route from Wilder's Square," beginning at page 109.)

Werner, Emmy, A *Conspiracy of Decency: The Rescue of the Danish Jews of World War II*, West View Press, 2002. (Note discussion of Henny Sinding at pages 66-68.)

Yahil, Leni, *The Rescue of Danish Jewry: Test of a Democracy,* The Jewish Publication Society of America, 1969.

Film Resources

Oral History Interview With Henny Sundø (formerly Henny Sinding), June 9, 1994, available at United States Holocaust Memorial Museum, Washington D.C.

The Power of Conscience: The Danish Resistance and Rescue of the Jews (containing an interview with Henny Sinding).

Appendix A

THE BOAT

Length Overall: 39 feet 9 inches
Waterline length: 35 feet
Beam: 14 feet
Draft: 5 feet 10 inches
Displacement: 20 tons
Propulsion System:
    Engine: Hundested Motorfabrik two cylinder "semi-diesel"
    Power output: 78 horsepower at 425 rpm.
    Engine weight: 7,055 pounds.
Estimated cruising speed: Eight knots
Built: 1926, at the Rasmus Møller shipyard in Faaborg, Denmark
Restored: 1992, at the J. Ring Andersen shipyard in Svendborg, Denmark

Gerda III *at Mystic Seaport.*
(Photograph courtesy of the Mystic Seaport Museum.)

Gerda III *on the Øresund with post-war colors.*
(Photograph courtesy of the Dragør Local Archive.)

Gerda III's *launching in Denmark.*
(Photograph courtesy of the Dragør Local Archive.)

Appendix B
THE CREW

The Crew

Gerda III's *crew servicing a buoy.*
(Photograph courtesy of the Dragør Local Archive.)

Crew member Otto Andersen.
(Photograph courtesy of the Dragør Local Archive.)

Appendix C

MAPS

*Denmark's Jutland Peninsula and
islands with surrounding countries.
(Drawn by Marjorie Rosenthal.)*

163

*Eastern shore of Denmark's Zealand
Island and neighboring Sweden.
(Drawn by Marjorie Rosenthal.)*

NOTES

1. Lidegaard, *Countrymen*, 329.

2. Ibid., 329-30.

3. *Gerda III, The Log of Mystic Seaport*, Summer 1997.

4. *Gerda III*'s wartime appearance and operating systems were restored by Denmark's J. Ring Andersen shipyard before it was transported across the ocean.

5. Werner, *A Conspiracy of Decency*, 85.

6. Two other rescue craft are known to remain afloat. One of these, a fishing boat named *Elisabeth K571*, is docked in Denmark at Dragør. Another, the schooner *M.A.Flyvberg* (now named the *Brita Leth*), continues to sail in Danish waters. The *M.A.Flyvberg* made a single crossing from Gilleleje, with 186 refugees on board, under circumstances that made it prudent to remain in Sweden until the war was over. The *M.A. Flyvberg* is discussed and shown in a photograph in Bo Lidegaard's *Countrymen*, 275-79. A third survivor of the rescue fleet, a 21 foot power boat used to great effect by the rescue and resistance group known as the Elsinore Sewing Club, is on permanent display in the United States Holocaust Memorial Museum in Washington DC.

7. Goldberger, *The Rescue of the Danish Jews*, 158.

8. Ibid., 158.

9. *Henny Sinding Oral History Interview,* United States Holocaust Memorial Museum ("USHMM").

10. Denmark—caught up in and ground down by the great power conflicts of the Napoleonic era—lost approximately one third of its population and two thirds of its territory in 1814, when Sweden pried Norway from Denmark's grasp after centuries of Danish rule. In 1864, after warring with Prussia for control of Schleswig and Holstein, territories that comprised a long-contested border region between Denmark and Prussia, Denmark was forced to cede both territories to Prussia. A portion of northern Schleswig rejoined Denmark following Germany's War World I defeat and a 1920 plebiscite.

11. Data concerning the number of Jews who lived in Denmark, and who survived or perished, are taken primarily from information published by the United States Holocaust Memorial Museum and, with respect to the number of Jews who escaped to Sweden, from recent data published at pages 329-30 of Bo Lidegaard's 2013 book *Countrymen.* The Jewish population figure includes 7,742 people who were transported to Sweden during the boatlift that began in the final days of September 1943, 470 who the Nazi's captured and transported to the Thereseinstadt Concentration Camp, 22 who drowned attempting to reach Sweden, 16 who committed suicide after the arrests began, and 5 who were killed as a result of their activities in the Danish resistance. The overall population figure also includes approximately 93 Jewish children who remained in Denmark, protected by Christian friends or relatives, after their parents had escaped or been captured.

12. Yahil, *The Rescue of Danish Jewry*, 42.

13. Lidegaard, *Countrymen*, 19.

14. Yahil, *The Rescue of Danish Jewry*, 54.

15. Ibid., 61.

16. Lidegaard, *Countrymen,* Author's Note.

17. The original cartoon by Ragnold Blix, was published in the January 10, 1942 issue of the *Gothenburg Trade and Maritime Journal.* A reprint appears at the start of Bo Lidegaard's *Countrymen.*

18. Yahil, *The Rescue of Danish Jewry,* 47-49.

19. Ibid., 50.

20. Steven Borish, *Hal Koch, Grundtvig and the Rescue of the Danish Jews: A Case Study in the Democratic Mobilization for Non-violent Resistance* (2009), 110-111.

21. Ibid., 110-111.

22. Yahil, *The Rescue of Danish Jewry,* 44-45, quoting an article entitled *"Denmark and Germany: Some Comments for People of Our Time on the Occasion of the New Year"* published January 1942 in *Berlingske Tidende.*

23. The Wansee Protocol used euphemisms in lieu of outright references to murder, but the meaning is clear. For example, the Protocol states that it will be "expedient" to deport Jews to labor camps where "a large proportion will no doubt drop out through natural reduction" and that any "remnants" will "require suitable treatment [lest they] become the germ cell of a new Jewish revival." Quotations of the Wansee Protocol are from the translation that appears on the website of Yad Veshem, The World Holocaust Remembrance Center.

24. Ibid.

25. Yahil, *Rescue of Danish Jewry,* 68.

26. Ibid., 61.

27. Ibid., 202.

28. Ibid., 202.

29. Ibid., 202-03.

30. Werner, *A Conspiracy of Decency*, 22-23.

31. Kieler, *Resistance Fighter*, 23-24, 32.

32. Mix's attempt to reach Sweden is recounted, in his own words, in a report that Kieler included in *The History of a Resistance Group,* Vol. 1, 105 to 108.

33. Werner, *A Conspiracy of Decency,* 29

34. Flender, *Rescue in Denmark*, 44.

35. Ibid., 47.

36. Werner, *A Conspiracy of Decency*, 33. Duckwitz's actions were recognized after the war. In 1955 he was welcomed back to Denmark as the West German ambassador. In 1971 his name was added to the list of the "Righteous Among the Nations"—a designation given to non-Jews who risked their lives to save Jews during the holocaust—at Israel's Yad Vashem holocaust memorial.

37. Werner, *A Conspiracy of Decency*, 26.

38. Werner, *A Conspiracy of Decency*, 39; Flender, *Rescue in Denmark*, 50.

39. Flender, *Rescue in Denmark*, 15.

40. Kieler, *Resistance Fighter*, 108.

41. Flender, *Rescue in Denmark*, 69; Goldberger, *The Rescue of the Danish Jews*, 6-7.

42. Levine, *Darkness over Denmark*, 101-102.

43. *Danish Patriots Renew Sabotage, New York Times*, October 5, 1943.

44. The identity of the "larger boat" that took Bohr on the final leg of his escape is not specified in Swedish arrival records or in published accounts of Bohr's escape and cannot be stated with certainty. An account that was handwritten in 1985 by a local archivist in Dragør, however, asserted that Bohr's "momentous flight" was organized by a resistance group led by Ejler Haubirk, Jr., the son of the Drogden Lighthouse keeper, and that it took place, at least in part, "in the lighthouse authority's boat"—a clear reference to *Gerda III*. The archivist, Svend Jans, was a twenty-one-year-old resident of Dragør at the time of Bohr's escape. Lending support to his account of *Gerda III's* involvement, other sources confirm that the "lighthouse authority's boat" performed missions for Haubirk's resistance group prior to the Jewish rescue operation when few other boats dared to do so. But Henny has disputed reports of *Gerda III's* role in Bohr's escape. And *Gerda III's* better documented missions prior to October 1 were limited to bringing resistance fighters to the Drogden Lighthouse—from which they would complete their crossing in a Swedish boat. *Gerda III* thus remains a possible, but unconfirmed (and in light of Henny's denial unlikely) link, in Bohr's escape.

The account of Bohr's escape on the *Søstjernen,* and his transfer to a second "larger boat," appears in David Lampe's *Hitler's Savage Canary,* at pages 80-81. Svend Jans' reference to *Gerda III's* role in the escape appears in a document in the Dragør Archives titled *Occupation-Relief Around Dragor 1940-1945,* May 5, 1985.

45. Flender, *Rescue in Denmark*, 76.

46. Werner, *A Conspiracy of Decency* at 83; Flender, *Rescue in Denmark*, 75-76.

47. Scientist Reaches London, *New York Times* October 9, 1943.

48. The daily arrival numbers were extracted from a bar chart appearing in Bo Lidegaard's *Countrymen,* 329.

49. Lidegaard, *Countrymen*, 255-56.

50. Werner, *A Conspiracy of Decency*, 76-77.

51. Goldberger, *The Rescue of the Danish Jews*, 101.

52. Ibid., 107.

53. Lidegaard, *Countrymen*,289.

54. Ibid.

55. Bettlesen, *October 1943*, 172.

56. Ibid., 169.

57. The numbers of Jews who were sent from Denmark to Theresienstadt is generally represented as either 464 or 474. Sources that site the lower number do not differ on the number of Jews who were arrested in Denmark. Instead, they engage in a netting out process, subtracting five prisoners of mixed religious heritage who Danish authorities managed to free from Theresienstadt in January 1944, and five others who are presumed to have died during transit. Goldberger, *Rescue of the Danish Jews*, 51; Yahil, *The Rescue of Danish Jewry*, 291.

58. Gerda III's activities prior to October 1943 are reported in Munkholt, *Ellen Wilhelmine Nielsen's Help in October 1943 to Jewish Refugees Fleeing to Sweden*.

59. Letter from Henny Sinding Sundø to Esther Blumberg and David Altshuler, Museum of Jewish Heritage, May 24, 1991; Werner, *A Conspiracy of Decency*, 67; Pundik, *In Denmark It Could Not Happen*, 109-110.

60. Henny's comments can be heard on a "Rescuers" video that runs continuously at the Museum of Jewish Heritage in New York.

61. Pundik, *In Denmark it Could Not Happen*, 109; Kieler, *The History of a Resistance Group*, 42 et seq.

62. Kieler, *The History of a Resistance Group*, Vol. 1, 42 et seq.

63. Pundik, *In Denmark it Could Not Happen*, 110; Werner, *Conspiracy of Decency* at 67.

64. The written recollections quoted in this paragraph appear in Herbert Pundik's *In Denmark It Could Not Happen*, 110 and in Kieler's *The History of a Resistance Group*, 42 et seq. The "1994 interview" refers to the Henny Sundø Oral History Interview in the research department of the United States Holocaust Memorial Museum.

65. Kieler, *The History of a Resistance Group*, Vol. 1, 42 et seq.

66. Ibid., 42 et seq.

67. On the fiftieth anniversary of the rescue Gert Lilienfeldt and Henny Sinding reunited on Gerda III and were interviewed by Danish journalist Marchen Jersild. Lilienfeldt's recollections of his escape on *Gerda III* and his earlier flights from the Nazis come largely from the resulting newspaper article, "Man Løber Bare" ("One Just Runs"), *Berlingske Tidende*, October 17, 1993.

68. The 320 "Aliyah" children between the ages of 14 and 16 who were brought to Denmark were placed in Danish homes to live, as part of the host families, during the occupation. The 377 older youths, who came to Denmark to learn farming skills that they could use to build a Jewish state in Palestine, lived in agricultural camps throughout the country. Lidegaard, *Countrymen*, 13. A total of 78 Jews from these groups, travelling an arduous route through Sweden, Finland, Russia and Turkey, made it to Palestine in 1940 and 1941. The Nazi invasion of Russia in 1941 cut off that route and completed the trap. Goldberger, *The Rescue of the Danish Jews*, 20-22.

69. Pundik, *In Denmark it Could Not Happen*, 110-11; Kieler, *The History of a Resistance Group*, 42 et seq.

70. Werner, *A Conspiracy of Decency*, 67-68; Kieler, *The History of a Resistance Group*, 42 et seq.

71. *Henny Sinding Oral History Interview*, USHMM.

72. Kieler, *The History of a Resistance Group*, Vol. 1, 42 et seq.

73. Goldberger, *The Rescue of the Danish Jews*, 5; Werner, *A Conspiracy of Decency* 48-50; Flender, *Rescue in Denmark* 118-122.

74. Goldberger, *Rescue of the Danish Jews*, 142-43.

75. *Resistance Fighter*, 96-99.

76. Kieler, *Resistance Fighter*. 96-97.

77. Goldberger, *Rescue of the Danish Jews*, 146-47.

78. Flender, *Rescue in Denmark*, 106.

79. Flender, *Rescue in Denmark*, 116-124; Werner, *A Conspiracy of Decency*, 48-50.

80. Kisling recorded his recollections, for the benefit of his family members, in 1971. A transcript of his recording, and related letters written by Kisling, were provided to me by one of his sons and they are the sources of all quotes that I attribute to him. The accuracy of his recording is supported by other sources, including a published comment by Mogens Staffeldt—a universally acclaimed leader of the Danish resistance—that Kisling was "one of the finest among us."

81. Flender, *Rescue in Denmark*, 105, 109, 114-15.

82. Ibid., 115.

83. *Mogens Staffeldt Oral History Interview*, USHMM.

84. Ibid.

85. Kieler, *The History of a Resistance Group*, Vol. 1, 42 et seq.

86. Ibid.

87. Weather data is extracted from the *Nautisk-Meteorologisk Aarborg* (Nautical-Meterological Annual) for 1943.

88. Ibid.

89. Dines Boge and Liv Thalov, *Dragør og St. Magleby Besat og Befriet* (Dragør and St. Magleby Occupied and Liberated), (1995), on file at the Dragør Local Archive.

90. *Gerda III*'s estimated speed of 8 knots (eight nautical miles per hour or about 9.2 statute miles per hour) is based on a surveyor's report prepared in 2000.

91. The destination was specified by Jørgen Kieler, as reflected in an interview memo on file at the Museum of Jewish Heritage.

92. Dragør's role in the rescue is comprehensively and excellently described in a research paper by Cherine Munkholt, entitled *Ellen Wilhemine Nielsen's Help in October 1943 to Jewish Refugees Fleeing to Sweden,* (2013), on file at the the Dragør Local Archives.

93. Munkholt, *Ellen Wilhelmine Nielsen's Help in October 1943 to Jewish Refugees Fleeing to Sweden*, 16.

94. Lidegaard, *Countrymen*, 289.

95. Ibid., 278.

96. Werner, *A Conspiracry of Decency*, 37-38. One expert on the Danish Rescue, Bo Lidegaard, has dismissed the notion that Camman suspended his patrols as a myth, unsupported by contemporaneous records. (*Countrymen,* 331.) But that ignores Duckwitz's writings which, in view of his other well established efforts to save Denmark's Jews, have considerable credibility.

97. Werner, *A Conspiracy of Decency*, 82.

98. Sixty one years earlier Burmeister & Wain built the Joseph Conrad, a three masted Danish training vessel that is docked a short distance from *Gerda III* at Mystic Seaport.

99. Kieler, *Resistance Fighter* , 57; Goldberger, *Rescue of the Danish Jews*, 143.

100. Kieler, *Resistance Fighter*, 72-73.

101. Ibid., 73.

102. Ibid., 122.

103. Kieler, *The History of a Resistance Group*, Vol. 2, 132 et seq.

104. Kieler, *The History of a Resistance Group*, Vol. 2, 132 et seq.

105. Kieler, *Resistance Fighter* , 73.

106. Kieler, *The History of A Resistance Group*, 132.

107. Ibid.

108. Flender, *Rescue in Denmark*, 230-31; Kieler, *Resistance Fighter,126-28;* Staffeldt Oral History Interview, USHMM.

109. Kieler, *Resistance Fighter*, 124.

110. Kieler, *The History of a Resistance Group*, Vol. 2, 132 et seq. Seventy years later, when visited by Mystic Seaport volunteer Nadia Jensen, Henny still had the pistol that Mix taught her to use and that she carried on her HD2 missions

111. Kieler, *Resistance Fighter*, 124.

112. *Henny Sinding Oral History Interview*, USHMM.

113. Flender, *Rescue in Denmark*, 225. In his warfare against the Nazis, as in his rescue work, Kisling's emergency vehicles were useful tools. They were, he stated in his recorded recollections, "just the right kind of [equipment] for sabotage operations." With such emergency vehicles "you can go out and place the bombs" while other vehicles were idled by the curfew, fuel shortages and other restrictions. Then, "you can come back with the fire engines or ambulances and see that the job is done well. If it is not done well, you can do quite a lot to make it well done."

114. Kieler, *Resistance Fighter* , 140 - 41.

115. Ibid.

116. Kieler, *Resistance Fighter*, 143-44.

117. Ibid., 148.

118. Kieler, *The History of a Resistance Group*, Vol. 1, 165.

119. Kieler, *Resistance Fighter* , 149.

120. Dr. Køster, hearing the shots as he approached his apartment, reversed course and avoided capture. After hiding for ten days in Denmark he was smuggled to Sweden on a schooner. Dr. Køster subsequently served as a medical officer in a British army unit that was among the first to enter the Bergen-Belsen

concentration camp in 1945. Kieler, *Resistance Fighter,* 145-46; Goldberger, *Rescue of the Danish Jews,* 147; Flender, *Rescue in Denmark,* 125-27.

121. Kieler., *Resistance Fighter* , 152-53.

122. Ibid., 158.

123. Ibid.,155.

124. Ibid., 158.

125. Ibid., 159.

126. Kieler, *The History of a Resistance Group*, Vol. 1, 200 et seq.

127. Ibid.

128. Kieler, *Resistance Fighter,* 161-67.

129. Kieler, *The History of a Resistance Group*, Vol. 1, 252 et seq.

130. Ibid., 253 et seq.

131. Ibid.

132. Ibid.

133. Ibid.

134. Ibid., 253, 264.

135. Kieler, *The History of a Resistance Group*, Vol. 2, 142-144

136. Ibid., 142.

137. The quotations in this paragraph are taken from the 1994 *Henny Sundø Oral History Interview* and from Kieler, *The History of a Resistance Group*, 42 et seq.

138. Against all odds Larsen survived and was reunited after the war with the "*02*" boat, which he then used as a pleasure craft for eleven years. Thanks in part to his post-war stewardship the boat became one of the few survivors of the rescue fleet, paving the way for its display in the Washington D.C.'s Holocaust Memorial Museum. Kiaer's rescue and resistance work, and Larsen's role in it, is wonderfully detailed by Birger Mikkelsen in *A Matter of Decency, the Resistance Movement's Sound Routes from Snekkersten and Espergaerde,* (1994), and by Flender in *Rescue in Denmark,* 153-65.

139. Steffensen's role in transporting weapons from Sweden to Denmark is described by Dragør historian Cherine Munkholt in *Ellen Wilhelmine Neilsen's Help in October 1943 to Jewish Refugees Fleeing to Sweden.*

140. Munkolt, *Ellen Wilhelmine Neilsen's Help in Octoner 1943 to Jewish Refugees Fleeing to Sweden,* 24.

141. Kieler, *The History of a Resistance Group*, Vol. 2, 192.

142. Kieler, *Resistance Fighter,* 334; Kieler, *The History of a Resistance Group,* Vol. 2, 198 et seq.

143. *Henny's Story,* Danish Defense Information and Welfare Service, (1945), 29.

144. Ibid., 30.

145. Flender, *Rescue in Denmark,* 247.

146. Kieler,*Resistance Fighter,* 286.

147. Goldberger, *Rescue of the Danish Jews,* 152-54.

148. Kieler, *Resistance Fighter,* 286.

149. Goldberger, *Rescue of the Danish Jews*, 11.

150. Werner, *A Conspiracy of Decency*, 112.

151. Ibid., 115.

152. Goldberger, *Rescue of the Danish Jews*, 154.

153. The 425 Jews who left Theresienstadt on the white busses included 417 Jews who had been deported from Denmark, three babies who were born in the camp, a Danish Jew who had been captured outside of Denmark, and four Czechoslovakian Jews who married Danes in the camp. Yahil, *Rescue of Danish Jewry*, 318; Werner, *A Conspiracy of Decency*, 120.

154. Werner, *Conspiracy of Decency*, 120-21; Goldberger, *Rescue of the Danish Jews*, 97.

155. The Danish Jewish Museum's research about the "hidden children" is well described in its publication: *Nothing to Speak of: Wartime Experiences of the Danish Jews 1943-1945*, by Sofie Lene Bak.

156. *Holocaust Encyclopedia*, United States Holocaust Memorial Museum website.

157. Yahil, *Rescue of Danish Jewry*, 278.

158. Ibid., 17.

159. The quoted portions of Professor Pelikan's writing appear in a chapter entitled *Grundtvig's Influence"* that he authored for Leo Goldberger's anthology, *The Rescue of the Danish Jews*.

160. Steven Borish, *Hal Koch, Grundtvig and the Rescue of the Danish Jews: A case Study in the Democratic Mobilisation for Non-violent Resistance,*115.

161. Goldberger, *The Rescue of the Danish Jews*, 162.

162. Lidegaard, *Countrymen*, 352.

163. The information described in this section was brought to light by Danish journalist and historian Jesper Clemmensen in his award winning book *Escape Route; Baltic Sea*, which was published in Danish in 2012. The English translation of Captain Gärtig's statement is taken from Philip Olterman's article, *Surfboards and Submarines: the Secret Escape of East Germans to Copenhagen*, which appeared in *The Guardian* on October 17, 2014.

INDEX

About the Author

IN 2009, HOWARD VEISZ left a 35-year litigation career and went to sea. After a two-year sailing voyage, he settled in Mystic Connecticut and began work as a shipyard volunteer at Mystic Seaport Museum, where *Gerda III*—Henny's Boat—is docked and cared for on behalf of the Museum of Jewish Heritage.

For much of the last decade, he has been deeply involved in preserving *Gerda III*, and in reconstructing the history of the boat and the people who put it to such good use. Working with his wife, the author travelled to Denmark to locate and meet with descendants, nephews and nieces of the people who carried out *Gerda III*'s rescue missions; gathered and analyzed writings by members of the *Gerda III* rescue and resistance group; scoured Danish archives; and visited the docks from which *Gerda III* and other rescue boats set out.

The author continues to play a leading role in preserving *Gerda III*, and is often invited to speak about the Danish Rescue and its lessons for today's world.

www.ingramcontent.com/pod-product-compliance
Lightning Source LLC
Chambersburg PA
CBHW060515130626
46553CB00002B/511